A daguerreotype of Dr. John McLoughlin taken late in his life. OREGON HISTORICAL SOCIETY

THE EAGLE & THE FORT

The Story of John McLoughlin

with all good wishes,

Dorothy Nafus Morrison

Dr. John at the height of his powers, painted by William Cogswell. *This portrait hangs over the mantel of the fireplace at the McLoughlin house.* MCLOUGHLIN MEMORIAL ASSOCIATION

Dorothy Nafus Morrison

THE EAGLE & THE FORT

The Story of John McLoughlin

ILLUSTRATED WITH OLD PRINTS
PHOTOGRAPHS & MAPS

WESTERN IMPRINTS
The Press of the Oregon Historical Society
1984

LIBRARY OF CONGRESS CATALOGING IN PUBLICATION DATA

Morrison, Dorothy N
The eagle and the fort.

Bibliography: p. 163
Includes index.
SUMMARY: A biography of the man who was the chief factor and developer of Fort Vancouver for the Hudson's Bay Company. Under his direction the fort became the center of settlement and civilization for the Pacific Northwest.
1. McLoughlin, John, 1784–1857–Juvenile literature.
2. Oregon–History–To 1859–Juvenile literature.
3. Northwest, Pacific–History–Juvenile literature.
4. Hudson's Bay Company–Juvenile literature.
5. Pioneers–Oregon–Biography–Juvenile literature. [1. McLoughlin, John, 1784–1857. 2. Northwest, Pacific–History] I. Title.
F880.M17M67 979.5'03'0924 [B] 78–12911
ISBN 0-87595-167-8

Lieutenant J. H. Warre made the drawing of Fort Vancouver (about 1845) that appears on the cover.

First edition (1979) published by Atheneum, New York City
Second edition (1984) published by
WESTERN IMPRINTS
The Press of the Oregon Historical Society

To the doctors in my family

Jim, John F., John M.,

And especially to

Carl,

For their compassion.

Contents

Author's Note

IN WRITING THIS BOOK I have used only real scenes and true dialog. Every conversation was really spoken, and somebody who was there wrote it down. Occasionally I have turned indirect quotations into direct ones, and I have quoted comments which people of the day recorded in journals and letters. I have had access to some which have never before been printed.

Three of Dr. John's important locales can be visited today: his Oregon City home, which is a national historic site and museum containing many of its original furnishings; Fort Vancouver in Vancouver, Washington, which is presently being restored by the federal government as a "living" fort, with costumed men and women busy at the old fur-trading occupations; and Old Fort William in Thunder Bay, Ontario, extensively rebuilt and also a splendid living fort. Visitors can see several other Hudson's Bay establishments which Dr. John founded, such as Fort Nisqually in Tacoma, Washington, and Fort Langley, near Vancouver, B.C. Part of York Factory on Hudson Bay is to be restored in the future.

McLoughlin is frequently pronounced as if the second syllable rhymes with "cough." *McLofflin.* However, in Canadian pronunciation which Dr. John used the second syllable ends with "awk." *McLawklin.*

I have many people to thank. First, Jean Morrison, Research Officer at Old Fort William, and Dr. John Hussey, author of *Champoeg: Place of Transition*, and *The History of Fort Vancouver*, for helping minimize the errors. These are both fine historians whose assistance I greatly value.

The staffs of Bancroft Library, Harvard University Press, Hudson's Bay Record Society, McLoughlin Memorial Association, Old Fort William, Oregon Historical Society, Public Archives of Canada, and University of British Columbia, in giving permission to use quotations from copyrighted or manuscript material, enabled me to make the book more interesting than it would otherwise be.

Thanks are due to dozens of scholars who patiently over the years have transcribed handwritten journals and letters into print, making my job easier. Many are included in the bibliography.

And finally I want to thank my editors Jean Karl and Marcia Marshall, and my friend Marian Martin, who helped shrink the manuscript to manageable length. They had what every book needs—good eyes for the essential, and sharp blue pencils for the rest.

Dorothy Morrison

THE EAGLE & THE FORT

The Story of John McLoughlin

ONE

The Flight

1784-1803

YOUNG John McLoughlin had to leave Quebec. He must turn his back on everyone and everything he knew, interrupt his brand-new medical career, go far away beyond hope of seeing his family and friends, perhaps for years. It would be hard. But he had lost his Scotch-Irish temper again, and this time was serious.

"It was entirely by my own want of conduct that I came up to this Country," he later wrote in a letter. "It was not a matter of Choice but of Necessity on my part."

John was eighteen, tall and strong, with piercing gray-blue eyes, a shock of sandy hair, and a booming voice. According to a family story, he and a lady friend had been strolling along a narrow street on a soft spring day of 1803 when they came to a plank laid over a mud-hole. Midway across, his friend in front, they met a drunken British officer in a red uniform with lace on his cuffs. The officer refused to go back. He shoved the lady off the plank. And powerful John, six feet four inches tall, stepped forward in a blaze of indignation, picked up the officer, and hurled him flat, to lie in the puddle with his magnificent epaulets, sword, boots and all, plastered with mud. In those days such an act was an insult to His Majesty's uniform, which might land John in trouble.

"There was danger in store for the young gallant," wrote the nephew who left the story. Its details may not be entirely accurate, but something of the kind happened—some "want of conduct"—that forced John to leave his home and all his friends and enter a strange, new, and often difficult life.

He had been born on October 19, 1784, in the village of Riviere du Loup, far down the St. Lawrence River. When he was quite small, his family moved to Quebec, after which he didn't see much of his father's people. They were substantial farmers of Riviere du Loup, landowners rather than tenants, but not very well educated.

He was better acquainted with his mother's relatives, the brilliant, quarrelsome, aristocratic Frasers. Grandfather Fraser, master of a handsome estate called Mount Murray, was forever starting squabbles. He briefly disowned John's mother for turning Catholic and marrying against his wishes, then gave her a farm and insisted that her children go to his own Church of

England. A brainy, warmhearted old man, he could speak several languages, and in spite of his interfering ways, John loved him.

Sometimes John and his younger brother David visited Mount Murray, where they saw men wearing kilts, heard them speaking Gaelic, listened to bagpipes. John would never forget them, nor his Highland heritage, nor his grandfather's long-drawn tales.

In 1798 John made a big decision for a fourteen-year-old—to become a medical apprentice. This meant that instead of studying at a university or working in a hospital, he learned by assisting his new master, in Quebec. He didn't use anaesthetics nor antibiotics, because they were not yet discovered. He didn't study bacteria, for doctors knew so little about infection that they sometimes sharpened their knives by stroking them across their boots. But his master was an eminent physician who taught John the skills of the time, such as how to set broken bones and to bleed his patients, which supposedly drew off poisons. Lanky young John must have spent long hours perched on a high stool while he ground herbs and rolled pills, and he probably drove his master's horse as it clop-clopped over the cobbled streets. He could hope for a fine medical career, but instead, after four and a half years, just about the time he finished his apprenticeship, he made the mistake that caused him to flee.

The question was, where should he go? Since his uncle, Simon Fraser, was a physician near Montreal, the worried young man asked him for help, and Uncle Simon promptly called on old Simon McTavish, head of the

Dr. Simon Fraser, the uncle who helped Dr. John get his job in the North West Company and later supervised McLoughlin's children while they were in school in the east. Dr. John corresponded with him until the uncle's death in 1844. MCLOUGHLIN MEMORIAL ASSOCIATION

Simon McTavish, one of the founders of the North West Company, who arranged young Dr. John's first job in the fur trade. PUBLIC ARCHIVES OF CANADA, OTTAWA

North West Company, fur-traders, whose headquarters were right there in Montreal. McTavish offered John a job the courts couldn't reach—a hard one in the far-off wilderness.

"A hundred pounds a year, if he is required to practice as a surgeon," McTavish promised Uncle Simon. "But I don't advise him to take it. If he goes on common wages, the company will take into consideration his time as apprentice to a surgeon."

"Meaning?"

"He'll get just a hundred pounds for the entire term. But he'll be bound for five years only, while others are bound for seven."

One hundred pounds—then a little less than five hundred dollars—was low pay for such a long time, but this plan offered a sure escape, so on April 26, 1803, John signed a long, elegant, hand-written contract, promising that for the next five years he would obey the company officers and go "whenever whereunto required and into any part of the Indian or Interior Countries." Because of McTavish's talk with Uncle Simon, John also thought he was to receive "expectations"—quick promotion—but these were not written down. Probably Uncle Simon didn't realize it was necessary.

While John was staying with his uncle he took his medical examination and received his license, and soon after that he was ready to start.

Since he was to travel with the yearly canoe brigade to Fort Kaministiquia on the farthest rim of Lake Superior, John went to the broad wooden North West Company wharves, where a crowd had gathered to watch them take off. The Ottawa River rolled at his feet, swift, clear, and blue-black except where it curled white over rocks. It would be a path to the unknown.

Canoes—huge canoes, thirty-six feet long, and wide and deep—rocked at the wharf, while dark-haired French Canadian *voyageurs* (canoe men) scrambled over them, balancing the packages of pork and peas and trading goods, and putting within easy reach the pitch and bark for repairs and sponges for bailing. As soon as they were loaded, John squeezed into place. All at once the crowd stopped talking. There came a breathless hush. A shout. The canoes pushed off, the voyageurs lifted their paddles and began their favorite song.

"*Rouli, roulant, ma boule roulant.*" (Roll along, my rolling ball.)

John had heard voyageurs' songs ever since he was a boy, and now—and now he was riding with them. Although this was not the doctor's career he had planned, it was exciting to start such a journey under the blue sky of spring.

Even a new apprentice-clerk was considered an officer, or "gentleman," so John didn't have to paddle. Instead, like the officers in other canoes, he sat in the middle, lanky legs doubled up, hardly daring to move for fear of poking his boots through the fragile birchbark.

The hours afloat were cruelly long, sixteen or eighteen per day, interrupted now and then for the voyageurs to pull out their white clay pipes, smoke a bit, and sing a paddle song. Every few miles they had to portage around a falls, or pull the canoes by ropes through rapids. When the riverbank was dangerous, the voya-

A large canoe, paddled by voyageurs *and carrying two "gentlemen," who wear beaver hats of felt made from the short underfur. Beaver hats, which were fashionable for more*

geurs leaped into the water and Dr. John unbent his cramped legs to ride ashore on the shoulders of a gallant little boatman. The voyageurs then unloaded the cargo, slung the ninety-pound packages on their backs—two or even three per man—and carried them at a dog trot up the trail, while Dr. John and the other gentlemen strode along behind. In an unbelievably short time they were underway again.

As they rode northwest through rivers and lakes, they were sometimes drenched by rain or stung by squalls of snow. When it was too stormy to venture onto the water, they huddled under upturned canoes beside blazing fires. Other days were hot, with sun and water a blinding glare.

Week after week they scudded on, farther from family and friends, deeper into the vast land of lakes and woods. At last, on an island near the western shore

than two hundred years, were the backbone of the fur trade.
HUDSON'S BAY COMPANY

of Lake Superior, they stopped to shave and change to clean clothes and unfurl the voyageurs' brightest ribbons. Now it was time for Dr. John to try to smooth his bedraggled coat, while the dignified senior officers opened the cassettes under their seats and put on their beaver hats.

Then, with the gentlemen sitting stiff-backed and stately, voyageurs singing, ribbons and pennants flying, the canoes swept into the huge blue circle of Thunder Bay, surrounded by forests, with rugged bluffs towering over all. A few hundred yards up the Kaministiquia River, past a thick stand of pine and birch, they came to an enormous timber wharf backed by the fort stockade of sharpened poles.

Strong brown arms steadied the canoe. Dr. John stepped out and climbed the wooden stairs, among barking dogs, brown-eyed children, and wintering employees eager for a bit of news.

He had reached his first wilderness post.

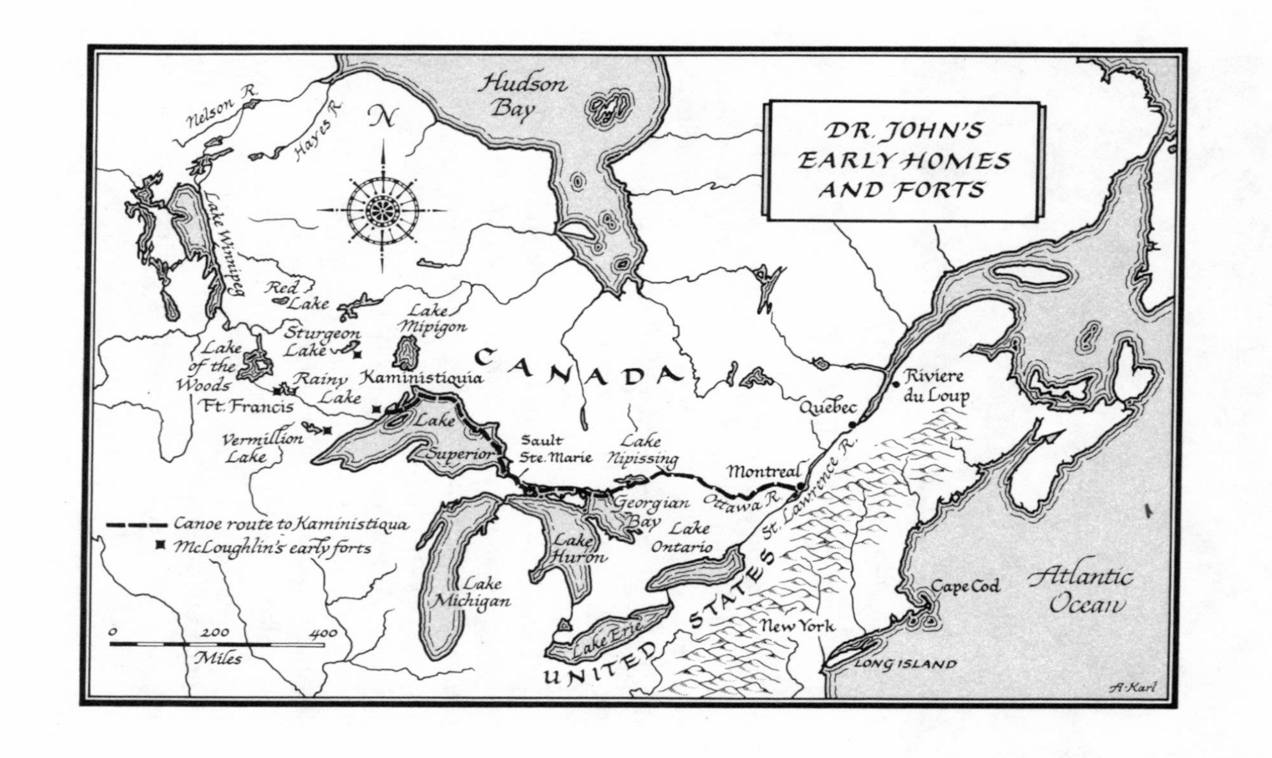
DR. JOHN'S
EARLY HOMES
AND FORTS
Hudson Bay
N
Nelson R.
Hayes R.
Lake Winnipeg
Red Lake
Sturgeon Lake
Lake Nipigon
Lake of the Woods
Rainy Lake
Kaministiquia
Ft. Francis
Vermillion Lake
Lake Superior
Sault Ste. Marie
Lake Nipissing
CANADA
Quebec
Riviere du Loup
Montreal
Ottawa R.
St. Lawrence R.
Georgian Bay
Lake Huron
Lake Michigan
Lake Ontario
Lake Erie
UNITED STATES
New York
Cape Cod
LONG ISLAND
Atlantic Ocean
Canoe route to Kaministiqua
McLoughlin's early forts
0
200
400
Miles
A. Karl

TWO

Lords of the Lakes and Forests

1803-1811

EVERY summer the men of the North West Company gathered at Fort Kaministiquia, later called Fort William. Voyageurs, laborers and Indians—fifteen hundred altogether—set up rowdy camps outside the stockade, while the gentlemen lived and worked inside. Dr. John met two kinds of officers: business agents from Montreal, who furnished capital, sold the furs and bought supplies; wintering partners, sometimes called "Lords of the Lakes and Forests," who lived on the frontier and traded with the Indians.

Summer was a time for big decisions and gargantuan feasts, and night after night, to the skirl of bagpipes, John joined the officers at dinner in the great hall. Dressed in tight-fitting trousers tucked into knee-high boots or gaiters, wide collars and ties, and long-tailed coats, they sat at two long tables and gorged on fish, beef, venison, milk and butter, bread, corn, peas, wine, ale, desserts—and, as special treats, moose nose, beaver tail and buffalo tongue. They ate a lot, laughed a lot, talked of faroff places and narrow escapes from bears and snows and white-water rapids.

They talked about their powerful rival, the Hudson's Bay Company, and about the United States, that upstart young nation that was buying almost a million square miles of land from France. Although this wasn't the place young Dr. John wanted to be, nor the life he wanted to lead, he was always interested in people and ideas, and no doubt he eagerly joined in. When the meal was done, the tables were cleared, and the gentlemen sang and danced until morning, while shouts of reveling voyageurs and Indians drifted through the windows.

Dr. John quickly got used to the bustle of the fort and the mixture of English, French and Indian tongues. The summer breeze off the lake was cool, smelling in the morning of wood fires and fresh-baked bread. Workmen and officers came to him for pills and potions and had him set their broken bones and bandage their wounds.

Even in the wilderness he tried to keep up with the times. "Let me know of any new discovery in medicine you hear of," he wrote to Uncle Simon, also asking for any historical books his uncle could spare, and sending him some petrified fir. Some day, maybe, he could go back to the civilized world.

For his first few years with the company, Dr. John was physician at Fort William during the summer gatherings, but in winter, when most men left, he took charge of a smaller post. Although the North West Company occupied many distant forts, Dr. John's were nearby in beautiful wooded country broken by thousands of clear blue lakes. There he bought all kinds of furs, but beaver was most important, for its soft under-hairs could be removed and made into the finest felt in the world. Beaver hats were expensive, treasured, handed down from father to son.

At these outposts he might go for months without meeting anyone who spoke English. He spent solitary, cold, uncomfortable days and nights in a drafty cabin, with deep snow outside, little to eat but game and fish, little to do. Leisure took up most of his time, and he longed to leave the monotonous lakes and forests and return home.

"When a man has been for any time in this Country he is entirely unfit for any other," he wrote. He spoke of "this sad Experiment," lamented, "I cannot accuse no one but myself of my bad fortune," and was so lonely that he once traveled by snowshoe two hundred miles each way to visit a friend.

Some time during these early years Dr. John married a Chippewa girl, probably in a typical fur-trader's marriage "by certificate." Since the wilderness had neither churches nor courts, some couples would merely begin living together, while others would go to the head

Fort William, painted in 1811, about the time Dr. John married Marguerite. The small structure with arched opening and pointed roof is the main gate. Next to it, on the right, is

the combined house-apothecary where Dr. John lived.
ONTARIO ARCHIVES, TORONTO

of the fort to sign a document with witnesses. Back in the settled area courts recognized such marriages as legal, and the company encouraged them because they helped keep the tribes friendly. Sometimes when they returned to civilization, the traders took these wives with them. Sometimes they left them with their tribes.

All we know of Dr. John's first wife is that she bore him a son, Joseph, and that later on another son said they were married by a Mr. McMillan. Since Joseph lived with Dr. John, it seems likely that the young mother died.

By the age of twenty-four Dr. John was a big, blustering man with bushy eyebrows and hair already turning gray. His friends considered him "an excellent companion," and he talked with them for hours in his booming voice, especially about his pet interest—history. But he missed his family, had never really wanted to be a fur trader, and often mentioned "going down"—leaving. His contract was nearly fulfilled. If he hoped to return to the city, now was the time.

However, in 1808, the year his apprenticeship ended, the summer express brought news that his brother David, who like John had been a medical apprentice, had gone to Edinburgh to finish his training. Although Uncle Simon had given him some money, it wasn't enough, and David was facing starvation.

All his life Dr. John was known for his great kindness, and now he was appalled at thought of his own young brother, alone in a foreign country, and in want. He was thinking about it when William McGillivray, the new head of the company, asked him to continue, but offered only one hundred fifty pounds per year.

Taken aback, Dr. John asked, "My prospects?"

"The same as any other young man," McGillivray replied. "That is, any other young man of character."

This didn't square with what Uncle Simon had said. "I understood otherwise," Dr. John insisted, "or I wouldn't have given five years of my time for the paltry sum of one hundred pounds."

Bitterly disappointed, he nearly decided to go and settle in Detroit. "I have but little to begin with but little will do," he wrote to Uncle Simon. "I prefer living on potatoes and milk . . . I will live in a Christian Country and live more happy than I do here." But if he attempted private practice, would he earn enough to help David?

He was still undecided when McGillivray called him in again and raised the offer to two hundred pounds a year, a difficult choice, for it would end his hopes of returning to civilization. Still, David needed help, so he accepted, and borrowed six months' pay in advance for his brother. "Had it not been for the money that I advanced David I would have gone down this year," he said.

Because he was generous, because he was kind, he had to stay in the wilderness. But he detested unfairness —to himself or to anyone—and he couldn't let go the dispute. In letter after letter, for four years, he complained about the greater pay of another medical apprentice and pestered Uncle Simon for the details of the agreement "as a satisfaction to myself."

As for David, although he was nearly thrown into

A HUDSON'S BAY COMPANY'S OUTPOST.

prison for debt, he eventually received his medical degree and became a surgeon in the British army.

About the time Dr. John decided to stay with the company, he made another decision, for he met calm, smiling, dark-eyed Marguerite McKay, part Chippewa and daughter of a Swiss fur trader. She had been the wife of Alexander McKay, a former North West partner who had resigned from the company, leaving her behind, and had gone to the Pacific Coast where he lost his life. Marguerite, who spoke a little French but mostly her native tongue, was charming and gentle, and Dr. John came to love her. He married her at Fort William, in a contract signed before the head of the fort, and took her with him to his next post, a "very poor" place on Vermillion Lake, in Minnesota.

Marguerite's even disposition was just what Dr. John's excitable one needed. Even though the soft snow fell day after quiet day, even though they had no one to talk with, and few comforts, they were happy in their rough log house at the lake. An intelligent man and interested in science, Dr. John wrote an essay on the neighboring Indians, and he may have explored the upper Mississippi Valley. But he spent only one winter free from worries. The next summer when he paddled back to Fort William, he found his company in trouble.

A typical fur-trading company outpost, with log building in a clearing at the edge of a lake. The figure at center is probably a trapper, in fringed leather suit, with a plume in his cap. OREGON HISTORICAL SOCIETY

THREE

The Great Fur War
1812-1824

IN that summer of 1812 Dr. John learned he would become a partner in two more years, which meant his voice would carry weight in the great hall, and he would be paid a share of profits instead of a salary. But he was restless in his frontier life. "I Still call Canada my home and reckon myself only as a Bird of Passage in this," he said. Being a partner brought status. It also brought worry because the Nor'Westers were clashing with an old rival, the Hudson's Bay Company, and the clash threatened ruin.

Away back in 1670 the King of England had given that company a charter over all the territory that drained into Hudson Bay—1,486,000 square miles, almost half the size of today's continental United States. The men of the North West Company insisted that the charter was only a scrap of parchment, because England had not owned all that land when it was issued, and besides, it had expired in 1697 and hadn't been officially renewed. Dr. John himself worked near the Great Lakes, but his friends boldly crossed Hudson's Bay territory on their way to the far west.

Now, however, a young Scot named Thomas Douglas, Earl of Selkirk, finagled an immense grant of Hudson's Bay land on the flat bare plains of the Red River near today's Winnipeg and planted a colony there. It straddled the canoe routes to the northwest fur lands, and the North-West brigades couldn't go around it because it was too large.

In the autumn of 1812, about the time Dr. John left for his winter's post, ragtag, hungry settlers began to arrive at the Red River colony. At first Dr. John's friends pitied them and fed them from the ample stores at their supply post, Fort Gibraltar. But this country had been home to generations of Metis, mixed-blood offspring of North-West traders and their Indian wives, and the Metis were angry and alarmed when the colony was laid out on their own lands. They fought skirmishes with the colonists and made threats.

Year after year, Dr. John watched the trouble deepen. In 1814 the governor of the Red River Colony forbade anyone to take provisions out of Lord Selkirk's grant. "You are to bark no trees for canoes or wigwams or cut large wood for camping," the governor told the Indians.

"Vacate all your posts!" he ordered the North

West Company. "Otherwise I shall raze them to the foundations."

The Indians, the Metis, Dr. John and his partners were furious, for the company had to have its routes and posts, or collapse. Fighting broke out everywhere, with both sides guilty. Metis burned settlers' barns, fired shots in the night and rode horses through crops. "Bay Men" seized a North West fort and stopped supply canoes. Dismayed at the senseless destruction, McLoughlin longed to leave, but hadn't the money.

Some of the partners egged on the Metis. Others, including Dr. John, felt things had gone too far and urged compromise. Many were convinced the Bay Men wanted to drive them out of business, and Dr. John was in despair.

"You cannot think how I long to go down," he wrote. "It makes my time appear long—I feel loansome, and quite low-spirited. People talk of the dessert of Siberia, but this is as bad."

At the summer gathering of 1815 trading goods were short, and tempers too. Ten winterers threatened to quit. When Dr. John was assigned to the Athabasca, far to the northwest, he shouted that he wouldn't go! Nor to Lake of the Woods! He'd throw up his share

Metis running buffalo, painted in the 1840s by Paul Kane. Buffalo meat was cut into strips, pounded to powder, and mixed with melted buffalo fat to make pemmican, which the Nor'Westers depended on to feed their men in the field. It was so nourishing that a hundred pounds would feed four men for a month. ROYAL ONTARIO MUSEUM

first! If he couldn't have a decent wintering post, he'd serve no more summers under the double load of physician and partner too.

"It seems [he] wont go anywhere unless he may chuse his Department," wrote a Montreal partner.

Finally, because they needed a doctor, the winterers kept McLoughlin at Fort William, probably in charge of the post, where he lived in his own combined house-apothecary shop (pharmacy) by the main gate. Compared to the outposts, this was luxury, for he had a birch bedstead, pine washstand, three green armchairs and some small pine tables.

However, to Dr. John's dismay, the conflict grew steadily worse. Governor Semple of the colony had North-West provisions seized and Fort Gibraltar burned, enraging both Metis and North Westers. Some of the partners wrote reckless letters. "A storm is gathering in the North ready to burst on the rascals who deserve it." "We will do our best to defend our rights!" "Here is at them with all my heart and energy."

Much as he longed for peace, Dr. John felt he must support his company in its fight for existence. In 1816 he started for Red River with several partners and five canoe loads of men. Before they arrived, the Metis killed Governor Semple and twenty-one colonists in a battle called the "Massacre of Seven Oaks." After meeting the Metis, Dr. John and the other partners paddled back to Fort William, where Lord Selkirk soon appeared with a hundred hired soldiers. He clapped Dr. John and the other partners under arrest and seized the post. Then, not feeling well, he returned to his own camp.

Left free, the North West partners spent a wild night. They smuggled a canoe-load of arms upriver, hid more in haylofts and concealed a barrel of gunpowder in a swamp. Upstairs and down they tramped with bundles of papers, and flames crackled in the kitchen fireplace as they burned documents that might incriminate them.

The next day when Lord Selkirk returned and saw the ashes, he angrily ordered the North West partners into canoes, to be taken east and tried. They later insisted that one canoe, McLoughlin's, was overloaded. On treacherous Lake Superior a sudden wind howled down upon them. Monstrous waves towered over Dr. John's craft. Voyageurs paddled frantically. Passengers bailed with anything—sponges, hats, bare hands. The canoe tossed, dashed them against its sides, until with a great rush of water it capsized. Nine men were drowned, and Dr. John was washed ashore "more dead than alive."

For a long time he lay inert on the sand while others worked desperately to revive him, and after he began to breathe, he was ill for many days. "Indeed at one time I thought I would have gone to the other world," he wrote.

Since his trial was delayed, he returned to Fort William, where he spent two long, weary years as its head officer. Finally, in October, 1818, he went to be tried at York, the capital of Upper Canada, now Toronto. Here he and five others were accused, not of the actual massacre, but of "receiving, relieving, comforting, or assisting the felons to escape."

It began one day and finished the next. He was not called to the stand, but sat as patiently as he could, a big, worried, white-haired man, watching intently with shrewd gray eyes while witnesses and attorneys argued about the massacre, and canoe routes, and the North West Company's need to feed its men in the field.

The jurors were out only forty-five minutes. "Not guilty," they said.

Dr. John was free.

But his face was troubled as he made the long canoe trip to Fort William and again took up the reins.

It was a dreadful time. Day after day came reports of stabbing, shooting, burning. One group died because they were cut off in the wilds without food. Dr. John was revolted by the cruelties. His company was facing disaster. He worried about money. Struggling to end the conflict, he wrote letters and set up meetings, for the wintering partners looked to him as their leader. When he couldn't get them relief through the Montreal agents, he considered switching the partners to the Hudson's Bay Company, which made the McGillivrays so angry they talked about "treachery in our camp," and removed him from his post at the head of the fort. This upset him. He tried, "by every means" to keep his position, but failed.

The Red River Settlement, painted in 1821, the year the North West Fur Company and Hudson's Bay Company merged. Colonists are fishing through the ice. On the knoll is the Nor'Westers' Fort Gibraltar, being rebuilt after the fur war. PUBLIC ARCHIVES OF CANADA, OTTAWA

By 1820 both companies were so near bankruptcy that they had to make peace or dissolve. Even though Dr. John no longer headed Fort William, the winterers still considered him their leader, so they sent him and Angus Bethune to London, to represent them, while William and Simon McGillivray went for the Montreal agents. It was a long crossing on a creaking slow vessel under sail, with coils of rope everywhere and icy winds whistling through the shrouds.

In London Dr. John met the Committee, was greatly admired, called an "honorable man" and "one of the few partners who had firmness of character." However, since William and Simon McGillivray were the official representatives, they were the ones who worked out the contract. In March, 1821, the two firms were united under a new charter that barred British competition from all lands where either had been trading.

From now on Dr. John's company—the new Hudson's Bay Company—would be run by the London Governor and Committee. No longer would he be part of the old free life of the "Lords of the Lakes and Forests." No longer would he join the banquets of moose nose and beaver tail at friendly old Fort William, for headquarters would be at bleak York Factory. He wouldn't even be called a partner, but Chief Factor (the top rank) or perhaps only Chief Trader. It was hard to accept. However, two important North-West practices were retained. The officers would share profits, and they would meet in the summer to make plans. This, at least, was a satisfaction.

Dr. John longed to strike out on his own, but he was caught short of cash. Besides Joseph, his son by his first wife, he and Marguerite had four children, Eloisa and David living at home, Elizabeth and John in school in the east. He had paid for their education, family expenses, his trial, travel to Europe. His North West account was overdrawn, and he would get no Hudson's Bay profits for three years, when the furs he collected were sold. So he was starting in a new company—in debt—with nothing coming in.

Receiving the top rank of Chief Factor, he was assigned a small post on Rainy Lake, with its countless blue waterways and forested shores. After his hectic years at big Fort William, he now knew isolation, silence, and the soft crunch of snow under his snowshoes. He gravely smoked with the Indians as he traded kettles and beads and blankets for the precious furs. The natives respected his height, his long white hair, his blustery ways and loud voice, and they trusted him because he was fair.

The United States–Canadian boundary at that point had been recently decided, but not yet surveyed, and American trappers built a strong post nearby. Even though they were his rivals, kind-hearted Dr. John cared for one of them who was injured, and he had his men search for two lost American children.

But he was an implacable business opponent, determined not to be outdone, so he put up three substations, out-traded the Yankees, and brought in a return. Company officers would be sure to notice this.

In spring 1824, when McLoughlin's canoes took

him to the summer gathering at York Factory, Marguerite, Eloisa and David went too. While the wind blew over the ice floes, officers met in the great bare hall to make decisions and hear where they were to be sent. Far down the list was remote Fort George at the mouth of the Columbia River, on the Pacific Coast. It was so distant, dangerous and costly that the Governor and Committee had thought of abandoning it, but had recently decided to hang onto it after all, in order to block Americans from the rich fur lands farther north. The leader for this risky post was finally named. "John McLoughlin, Chief Factor."

This was no light assignment. It was difficult—important. And instead of going down, as he still longed to do, Dr. John must move even farther from the civilized world.

FOUR

To the New Fort

1824-1825

DR. John and Marguerite began a flurry of packing. Of all the children they would take only six-year-old Eloisa and three-year-old David, for the others were too far away. However, George Simpson, in charge of the northern section of the Hudson's Bay Company in America, was to go along.

In his late thirties, a short, stocky man with sandy hair, he was called "Governor," a title which was also used for the top Hudson's Bay officer in London. Governor Simpson was a no-nonsense dynamo who would sacrifice anything or anyone—including himself—for the good of the company. Legend says he once goaded his voyageurs until one seized him by the collar, lifted him into the water, and held him there until he agreed to slow down. He worshiped efficiency, slashed the number of employees, reduced wages, closed posts that didn't pay. One writer called him a "cold, calculating machine . . . a most effective machine, but not a truly noble man like McLoughlin." And yet he was loyal to his men. Once, when one died and as a last wish asked to be buried among his own people, Simpson put the body into a keg of rum and took it back in his own canoe, to make sure the superstitious voyageurs wouldn't throw it overboard. The governor and Dr. John were going to be associates for a long time.

Although Dr. John was ready, Simpson was waiting for instructions from the London Governor and Committee. Day after day lookouts climbed the wooden tower and gazed toward the bay with its scattering of ice floes. No sail appeared. Finally they decided that Dr. John with his family could not risk the winter's snow, but should start at once with two canoes. Simpson would wait for the ship, travel light, and try to catch up.

On July 27 Dr. John, Marguerite, David and Eloisa stepped aboard and waved to watchers on the wharf. They headed up the marshy Hayes River, rounded a curve, and the fort was out of sight. Three weeks later, with the ship still not arrived, Governor Simpson started out in a single canoe.

Dr. John and Marguerite, with two small children to care for, wound interminably through dark forests or plodded over portage trails, moving away from friends, deeper into the unexplored wilderness. They endured cold, fogs, storms, rivers so low the voyageurs had to drag the canoes through oozing mud. Portages slowed them. The food was monotonous, canoes were cramped, and mosquitoes a torture.

Two long months after they started, they were overtaken by Governor Simpson. By this time Dr. John's once-fashionable clothes were covered with a thousand patches of different colors—probably sewn on by Marguerite.

"He was such a figure as I should not like to meet in a dark night in one of the bye lanes in the neighbourhood of London," wrote Simpson, adding that he was "loaded with Arms," that "his beard would do honour to the chin of a Grizzly Bear," and that the total effect "would convey a good idea of the high way men of former Days."

They went on together. At dread Athabaska Pass over the northern Rockies they cached their canoes for some party going the other way, and mounted horses. Drenched by rain, they toiled upward for seven days, as cliffs and glaciers hung above them and the Athabasca River roared beside the trail. However, once they came to the top the descent was quick, and on October 19, Dr. John's fortieth birthday, they reached the northernmost loop of the Columbia River, in today's British Columbia. There a party from Fort George was waiting with two boats and a cedar canoe.

Now began a wild three weeks' dash downstream, past gorges and sheer cliffs, sagebrush plains, bare hills. Near the Cascade Mountains, they portaged around a thundering waterfall where Indians were fishing with dip nets. From here on the banks were lined with native villages. Men were catching salmon or scraping out

Tracking a fur-company canoe, which has been unloaded to lighten it, so it can be drawn up the rapids. At center left some of the voyageurs are carrying bundles on their backs. If the

rapids were very dangerous, they would also carry the canoe.

THE NATIONAL GALLERY OF CANADA, OTTAWA

canoes, while women smoked fish over long fires or wove baskets and hats. They were well fed, good humored, friendly. Even when one McLoughlin boat accidentally rammed a native canoe, the Indians were not angry, but swam around "like seals" and laughed heartily.

Gradually the bare hills became dotted with juniper, with scattered pine, and finally with jungle-thick forests. The travelers passed gray crags and steep banks laced with waterfalls. And at last they wearily rounded a final bend and pulled up to the wharf at sunset on November 8. After more than three-and-a-half months, Dr. John's trip was done.

Now he could see Fort George, which he had come so far to command—only a forlorn little post after all, on a knoll surrounded by huge swaying trees. The wide gate swung open for the bedraggled group to enter the stockade and be fed, and sleep in beds—their first since York Factory, an eternity ago.

During the next weeks, while the gray rain fell, Dr. John struggled with a host of new problems. He had to learn Chinook jargon, the mixture of English, French and Indian tongues which was used for trade all up and down the Columbia. His neighbors, the intelligent Chinooks under old one-eyed Chief Concomly, were

Fort George as it looked when Dr. John arrived there. Its buildings are connected by palisades of sharpened poles to form a protected courtyard. A towering forest surrounded this fort for miles. OREGON HISTORICAL SOCIETY

PARSONS. DEL.
AVERY. SC.

friendly, but more distant tribes were not. The Columbia Department was losing money, partly because the warehouses held such improbable items as ostrich plumes and coats of mail, partly because space in the tiny supply ships had been squandered in bringing all the men's food. As Simpson gloomily remarked, "All this time they may be said to have been eating gold."

Besides making a profit, Dr. John was supposed to keep Americans away from the Columbia. No country really owned this land, for the Canadian boundary was decided only to the Rockies. West of that, Alaska belonged to Russia, and California to Mexico, while England and America both claimed the largely unexplored territory between. Since they couldn't agree how to divide it, they had it in "joint occupancy," which gave citizens of both countries the right to settle and trade there. This was an invitation to trouble.

Dr. John also had to find a permanent post, because Fort George didn't really belong to the British. Americans had built it, lost it in the War of 1812, and recovered it by treaty after the war. The Yankees weren't sure they wanted to win the west coast, so distant, and cut off by mountains and desert. One senator said, "Oregon can never be one of the United States. If we extend our laws to it, we must consider it a colony." So they were letting the British use Fort George, but they could reclaim it any time, and knowing this, the London Committee wanted a new post built on the north bank of the river.

However, the area was soaked by torrential rains, open to attack from the sea, and covered by gigantic

A big tree near Fort George, drawn by the Wilkes expedition, 1838, with an instrument which projects an image onto paper so it can be traced. Trees of the coast grew to immense size, which made it difficult to clear fields for raising food.
OREGON HISTORICAL SOCIETY

trees which would have to be cleared before much food could be raised. Simpson and Dr. John agreed that they should leave the area, but they didn't agree about where to go. Simpson wanted the main fort to be farther north on the Fraser River, and sent men there to explore. Dr. John was interested in finding a suitable site on the Columbia.

Up and down the river his big frame toiled, along banks that were either steep and rocky, or low and liable to flood. He hacked his way through tangles of fragrant red cedar, stiff-leaved salal, ferns as high as a man. He spent long days in a canoe. Once, when he and Simpson were out in a boat, the rotten rigging let the sails come down around their ears, and they nearly drifted to the open sea, but the tide turned just in time to bring them back to shore.

At last, nearly a hundred miles upstream, near the mouth of the Wal-a-mot River (later spelled Willamette) Dr. John found a slope that overlooked parklike plains and timber and lakes. To the east was the snow-capped peak of Mt. Hood. This place had everything he wanted—beauty, safety from attack, open land for farming, and ample rainfall. He wrote to London, "Immediately on Mr. Kennedy and my Return to Fort George from upstream, a party was sent to begin building . . . we found no eligible situation to Build on nigher the Entrance of the River."

He soon had boats and canoes carrying goods up the Columbia. Fort George owned a few goats, cows, oxen and ponies, for which he had his men build a large, ungainly flat-bottomed craft with masts and sails. One day when the wind was upriver, he had the excited animals loaded on the great ark, and started off.

On Wednesday, March 16, the friendly Chinook Chief Concomly waved sadly from shore as Dr. John, Governor Simpson, and most of the company set out in four heavily laden boats. They passed dark fir forests, occasional sandy beaches, and the Island of the Dead, where burial canoes were fastened to the trees. They saw a few eagles, many deer.

For two nights they camped, and on Friday they landed below the fort. Proudly Dr. John strode up the long slope to the fresh-cut palisade, about a mile and a quarter from the water. This was his fort, but not his only one, for Simpson had given him full charge of the entire Columbia District, including several widely scattered smaller posts.

The double gate swung open. Inside stood only a rough dwelling for himself and his family, tents and bark huts for the people, a couple of stores, and an Indian hall. Roofs were of boards, not shingles; nothing was painted; most floors were of earth. But Dr. John planned far more. From this spot he would direct the trade, the personnel, the policies, of this whole coast. Indians, traders, sea captains, adventurers—all would come to him here. Simpson was wrong, he thought. This was the place for headquarters, not the Fraser.

The next day everyone got up early. As sunrise lighted the sharp tips of the stockade, the gentlemen, servants, chiefs and Indians gathered in the yard, where Simpson broke a bottle of rum on the flagstaff and declared in a loud voice, "In behalf of the Hon'ble Hudson's Bay Company I hereby name this Establishment Fort Vancouver. God save King George the Fourth." This name, for the first Englishman to send boats into the Columbia, had been chosen to strengthen the British claim to the area.

After three loud cheers and a couple of drams of rum all round, everyone walked down to the waterfront. Governor Simpson lowered his stocky frame into place. Paddles set up glittering spray. The canoe darted across the water. As it dwindled toward the misty cone of Mt. Hood, the song of voyageurs drifted back.

"Rouli, roulant, ma boule roulant."

And then—the canoe and the song were gone. Dr. John was on his own.

FIVE

Getting Started

1825-1829

FOR the time being Dr. John didn't finish Fort Vancouver because he simply couldn't stretch his manpower to do everything, and raising food came first. So he had his men break the prairie sod below the fort and plant his only seeds—two bushels of peas, some potatoes, and a few beans. The farm animals would have to find their own shelter and food.

From the fort gate Dr. John could see the small fields on the flats below, with the mighty river just beyond. The spring sun was warm. It shone on the rough buildings and drying puddles of the fort yard, while the air was fragrant with new-cut wood.

His crops grew fast. After his first harvest he reported with satisfaction, "Our farming is coming on as well as we could expect, except in Pigs, of which we have lost four large since last Spring poisoned by eating a kind of poisonous Camas." A few other pigs had been devoured by wolves, but the fort had raised good amounts of "pease" and potatoes.

For all his hard-won success, he hoped to go down "in about three years."

"I cannot say that I admire much this country," he wrote. "Since my Arrival on the 8th of Novr we have not seen one clear sun Shineing day and not ten days without rain."

Something—David's needs, the fur war, his debts—always seemed to lock him into the fur trade. Now, even though he was at last receiving a share of profits, his account was still overdrawn, which required him to stay until he could clear it up. But surely in three years. . . . Although his son Joe, who had been left behind, came to him overland, Dr. John hoped none of his family would be on the Columbia for long. Once he was so near leaving that Marguerite and the children actually started out with a brigade, but turned back at the Rockies because he sent word he had changed his mind.

New challenges constantly arose. One summer day he received a report from Peter Skene Ogden, who was leading a fur brigade in the desolate Snake River country. Ogden said that twenty-three "free men," who were paid by the skin rather than on a salary, had deserted.

"We have long wished for an opportunity to join the Americans," they had said. "We have now been five Years in your Service, the longer we remain the more indebted we become. We are now in a free Country and have friends to support us, and go we will."

Dr. John was first angry, then troubled, for he knew what a hard life these men led. He knew they slept out in leather tents, constantly waded in ice-cold streams, set their traps underwater with numbed hands, and sometimes went for days without food. He knew that some of them died. So he added up returns and costs and found that the company was paying so little for skins and charging so much for supplies that a man who made a large catch could barely make ends meet, while a moderate one would leave him mired in debt. Profits per skin were large, the company needed the trappers, and if McLoughlin asked the London Committee for advice, a year or more would drag by before he got an answer.

Therefore, deciding to take things into his own hands, he set up new rates—ten shillings per beaver instead of two, and cheaper supplies. He might be running a risk. The Governor and Committee might not approve. But the old system wasn't fair, and he was determined that anyone working for him should receive justice.

As he had hoped, the year the new rates began, Ogden reported that not a single trapper deserted, and when the Committee's reply finally came, it was favorable. "We can afford to pay as good a price as the Americans," it said.

For the first time Dr. John had boldly changed Hudson's Bay policy.

Ships and their captains were another trial. In April, just after he moved into the new fort, the white-winged

Trappers, painted by John Jacob Miller in 1837. Such men were often on the frontier for years. The painter said these had made their own hats, and Indian women had sewn their fringed leather suits, using animal sinews for thread.
WALTERS ART GALLERY, UNIVERSITY OF OKLAHOMA

William and Ann sailed into the Columbia River after rounding the Horn—Cape Horn at the tip of South America. Since no one knew how far upstream ships could sail, she anchored near Fort George, while her supplies were brought to Fort Vancouver in boats.

Dr. John desperately needed those supplies, but his heart sank when he learned how wet they were. "We will lose about a seventh of the Flour and Meal," he wrote the Committee, and added that the gunpowder was "damper than any we have hitherto had," the pork and beef "not so good," the barrels "very bad," and the bricks "very inferior."

Besides that, the ship herself needed repairs, so Dr. John sent his hard-pressed men downstream with hammers and saws and kegs of pitch. By June she was seaworthy again.

He then told her captain, Henry Hanwell, to sail north, explore the waterways, and "undersell any Trader he found on the Coast." He knew those waters were crisscrossed by Yankee ships called "coasters," which might leave if the British could monopolize the furs. As the ship set out, Dr. John hoped and believed he had begun a thriving trade with the north.

About the time the vine maple turned red along the edge of the forest, the ship returned. But her trip had failed. Captain Hanwell had been terrified of the Indians, terrified of the narrow inlets where frost-green glaciers hung on the mountain sides. He had refused to enter the bays, failed to locate river mouths. When a friendly American skipper offered to show him how to adapt his ship to the trade, Hanwell declined. He had secured few furs and scant information about the natives. Worse, he had weakly given the Indians liquor, which made Dr. John's eyes blaze with anger.

"We sell no liquor to them on any account," he sternly told the luckless captain. "Selling liquor to Indians is prohibited by a positive order of the Committee."

He hadn't achieved his longed-for trade with the north, but he still received no authority over ships, although he pleaded for it.

His job became even more complex when the Governor and Committee added a huge sweep of the far north to his district, making him responsible for the entire coast from California to Alaska, and from the Rockies to the Pacific. Now he had still more forts to manage. He must see that they all had food and trading goods, tools and ammunition, and that their officers ran them well. He was constantly dictating orders, sending or receiving shipments, and transferring men.

The London Committee didn't send his supplies long enough ahead. When one vessel was late, he couldn't afford to give the Indians traps because if they caught many animals, the forts wouldn't have articles to trade for the skins. They had no bags for carrying corn to their forts. Medicine was short—and beads—and blankets. He had to lend his own gun to the leader of a brigade.

"Of course this must be kept a secret even to our own people," he cautioned his officers.

Worse than the ships, the skippers were bunglers, drunkards, cowards, or dishonest. One irritated the Indians until they nearly went on the warpath, while several traded with them illegally.

McLoughlin wouldn't give up. In report after report he explained his problems with captains and pleaded for goods to be sent a year ahead. He tried to build two ships, but their seams opened. Finally the Committee assigned three vessels to him, one coming from London each year, one returning, and one staying on the coast. This would help a little.

One skipper brought an unexpected dividend—a handful of apple seeds—a treasure. Dr. John had them planted in small boxes and kept under glass until they were large enough to be set out. He himself watched over the tiny orchard, to be sure no one touched it, and the day the first apple was ripe he was so elated he called for his daughter Eloisa.

"Now come and see, we are going to have some apples," he said, his ruddy face beaming, as he carefully cut the single fruit so the family and gentlemen could each have a taste. It was a treat.

The farm continued to expand. By 1829 it had two hundred hogs and fifty goats, but cattle were so scarce that Dr. John didn't allow any to be butchered except one calf yearly for rennet, which they needed to make cheese.

After several crops of wheat had been planted and saved for seed, his fort finally had a surplus for making flour. At first his workmen merely hollowed out a great stump to hold the wheat, then pounded it with a spring pole that worked a heavy pestle. But before long a seventy-year-old blacksmith named Cannon made a real mill that used stones and was turned by eight oxen, plodding around a circle.

Dr. John was everywhere. Fashionable gold-headed

Most of the pictures of Dr. John are not dated, but this is among the earlier ones. His hair had turned white when he was young. OREGON HISTORICAL SOCIETY

cane in hand, he walked through the fields, supervised workshops, checked furs, kept track of supplies at all forts, dictated mountains of reports and letters, or wrote them out himself in the big brown leather letter books for the clerks to copy. Sometimes, when a man displeased him, he stamped up and down, thumping his cane and muttering threats, while Marguerite sat nearby, placidly knitting, with needles clicking softly and sounds of the fort in the background. Having her there, so quiet and calm, soothed him as nothing else could.

He was proud of the progress, and rightfully so, for this establishment was far different from the weak little Fort George he had found not many years before.

"Mr. Ogden's returns are better than last year," he wrote, referring to the Snake expedition. And again, "Our crops look uncommonly fine, is now cutting and part Housed." "With the Flour we now had and our Wheat I think we will have a years stock of this article in advance."

Dr. John tried anything that might turn a profit. Once when the fur brigades went out to trade, he said, "I sent a share of every Trading Article in the Store, so as to find a Market for Several articles which are a dead Stock on our hands." This probably included the ostrich plumes and coats of mail he had found at Fort George.

He also shipped to London three swan skins and some isinglass to see whether they were worth collecting. He sent salmon to California and the Sandwich Islands (Hawaii), and, finding markets there for lumber too, he had a water-powered sawmill built a few miles upstream. By 1829, after only four years on the coast, he had begun the major industries of today's Northwest—lumber, salmon, fruit, wheat and water power.

Fort Vancouver was on its way.

SIX

The White-Headed Eagle

1828-1829

IN order to succeed on the Columbia, Dr. John had to keep peace with the Indians. He was helped in this by the Hudson's Bay monopoly, which made it good business to be friends with the natives. Company officers saw that their employees obeyed the rules, let tribes keep their customs, and sold them medicine, blankets, guns, kettles and shirts. When Hudson's Bay men married Indian girls, they were generally good husbands. The company was firm, but it didn't offer rewards for scalps or punish the innocent for the crimes of a few.

He was also helped by the company policy not to settle the land, but keep it a fur-bearing wilderness, which was what the Indians wanted, too.

Still another aid was Dr. John's kind, fair nature.

Many Indians worked at Fort Vancouver. Once, when one committed a serious offense, he was brought to Dr. John, who asked, "Is he guilty?"

"Yes."

Dr. John pointed to an artillery piece standing in the courtyard. "Tie him to the cannon," he ordered. "Give him fifteen lashes." When a white man did the same thing, he received the same punishment. In those days flogging was common, and the tribes were impressed because their own man was handled the same as the other.

Eloisa said, "The whites themselves sometimes troubled the Indians and then they complained to my Father. He put men in irons who treated the Indians badly."

As a result, most Indians liked the British. Sometimes on Sunday they gathered outside the fort stockade to sing and dance in rings, and once, when an upriver fort was to be moved, the neighboring Wascos sent out a hundred war canoes to try to force the company to leave "their" fort in place. Instead of punishing them, Dr. John impressed them with his roaring cannon, gave them presents and a feast, and sent them back, still friends.

But it wasn't always so easy. One night in August, 1828, when he had been on the coast for three years, Dr. John was awakened by a noise at the gate. Sleepily he pulled on some clothes and hurried to his office, where a guard had admitted a haggard white man, brought by a band of Tillamooks. At first the stranger

An Indian woman of the Cowlitz tribe with her baby. Many Indians of the coast flattened their heads by binding infants for several months between cradleboard and a piece of bark. A flat forehead was a sign of aristocracy, only the slaves being left round-headed. Oddly, the tribe called "Flathead," living inland, did not do this. The woman in this picture died soon after the sketch was made, and her friends thought the artist had caused her death by taking her likeness.

ROYAL ONTARIO MUSEUM

was too exhausted to speak, but finally he managed to say he was Arthur Black, an American from a party under Jedediah Smith. On the Umpqua River, two hundred miles south, a group of Kelawatset Indians had stolen the American's axe.

"It was the only axe we had, and we needed it to make rafts," Black said. "So we took the chief prisoner."

They had bound him and held him until the axe was returned.

The next morning Jed Smith and two men left camp to find a ford across the river. While he was gone, Indians attacked the camp and killed most of the men.

Dr. John had traded with the Kelawatsets and found them friendly and dependable, and he privately thought the Americans had invited trouble by humiliating the chief. But he felt duty-bound to defend the Yankees, even though some of his officers objected.

"The honor of the whites is at stake," he said. "If we do not succeed, it will be dangerous to be seen any distance from the fort . . . The next attack might be on one of our own parties."

So he rewarded the Indians who had brought in Black, and sent runners south with gifts of tobacco for friendly chiefs, asking them to search for the missing Jed Smith. Just as he was ready to send out a rescue party, Smith himself and two tattered men arrived. They said that besides killing the men, the Kelawatsets had taken all their goods.

Since Chief Trader Alexander McLeod was about to lead a fur brigade south, Dr. John told him to find out what had happened, and recover Smith's property.

The Indians told the trader that Smith's men had repeatedly insulted the Kelawatsets, and had boasted that they would drive out the British. He also found that Smith's belongings had been sold to both Umpquas and Kelawatsets, and were widely scattered. McLeod had bungled one expedition. This time Dr. John gave him written orders, and guided by these, the trader persuaded an Umpqua chief to move with him from place to place, not making war, but peacefully seeking Smith's property. He made it clear that none of the British would buy stolen goods, and that unless the tribes turned them over, they would receive no favors.

Years later Dr. John explained that when the Indians demanded pay for the furs and equipment, McLeod asked, "Pay? To murderers?"

The Indians denied killing to obtain the furs, saying, "We bought them."

"Then look to the murderers for payment."

This, Dr. John said, made the Indians angry, not at his men, but at those who had sold them stolen skins. The Indians themselves punished the guilty, and without starting a war, the British recovered most of the property.

"It was done," he said, "from a principle of Christian duty, and as a lesson to the Indians.

As for Jed Smith, he was so grateful that he had his company stop trapping west of the Rockies, to avoid competing with Dr. John. He also sent east a detailed report of the Hudson's Bay fort, with its workshops, livestock, wheat and orchards. People in the clapboard houses of New England, the cabins of the prairies, heard about his report and thought it over. Maybe they ought to pay more attention to this wild Northwest.

Other Indians were hostile that year. One group killed five Hudson's Bay men who were traveling in the north, and a coastal tribe seized the cargo of a wrecked ship. Dr. John had them both punished, but when one of his expeditions killed a large number of innocent natives, he was so angry that he blocked the promotion of its leader.

By now tribes all up and down Columbia River knew Dr. John for his towering rages, his firmness, and his fairness. They knew he wouldn't let his men slaughter innocent natives, but that he wouldn't be cheated, and that it wasn't safe to kill any whites, not even the Yankees. When he first came to the Columbia, travelers had to go well guarded, but after a few years, his brigades needed only enough men for portages. Although he still had Indian trouble at times, it involved distant tribes. The ones nearby trusted him—loved him—feared him. "The White-Headed Eagle" they called him, and as such he kept the peace.

During all his years on the Columbia there were no Indian wars.

SEVEN

A Greater Fort Vancouver

1828-1829

IN 1828 Governor Simpson came on a tour of inspection. Energetic and dignified as ever, he traveled in full glory with bagpiper, singing voyageurs, and a gorgeous cloak of red Scottish plaid with a scarlet lining.

Still thinking about the Fraser River, he had come that way and found sheer rock walls, ferocious rapids, and places where he had to go over hanging rope ladders put up by the Indians. For traders, he said, the river would be "certain Death in nine attempts out of Ten."

Ever since the governor had first planned to move to the Fraser, Dr. John had conscientiously found out all he could about it. He had more than once warned the Committee that it was "difficult and dangerous," or "unnavigable," and now he was proven right. He was overjoyed because he could keep his beloved headquarters and build for the future. He wouldn't be uprooted.

The tall Chief Factor and the stocky, energetic, little governor had a busy time. They tramped around in the winter rain or went by horse and canoe to inspect everything—fields, orchards, sawmill. They claimed a site at the falls of the Wal-a-mot, forty miles south of Fort Vancouver. At night, working by candlelight, they figured profits and costs, trading goods and transportation.

The governor was especially delighted because "eatables and drinkables" no longer filled the supply ships. He praised McLoughlin's judgment, and in his private notebook he called Dr. John "a very bustling active man who can go through a great deal of business," and "a good hearted man and a pleasant companion." But a sour note must have been struck somewhere, for Simpson also wrote that "a difference of opinion almost amounts to a declaration of hostilities." It was only a hint. The real trouble hadn't yet begun.

Early in 1829 Simpson left, so Dr. John was again in full charge. Knowing that his post was permanent and that he didn't need high ground for defense against Indians, he decided to move to a spot closer to the river. Here he built a new fort that became famous as an island of luxury in the wilderness, where candles gleamed in silver candelabra while gentlemen and guests ate elaborate dinners on blue and white dishes from England.

The courtyard bell ruled the day. On summer mornings when it rang at five, the fort came to life with the sound of hammers, clang of anvils, rumble of carts and shouts of workers. At eight it rang for breakfast and at noon for dinner. Then the men in the field turned out their oxen, clerks hurried across the yard to the gentlemen's dining hall, fur beaters laid down their flails and went to their crude cabins by the river. At one the bell clanged again to call them back to work until six. On Saturdays they gathered in the courtyard to receive their week's rations—five gallons of potatoes and five salt salmon per man, plus a few "pease" and some tallow. They counted on Indians' hunting and fishing for other food.

Every day Dr. John walked from shop to shop, to the forge, the gardens, the bakery. He sampled the tough unleavened biscuits, talked with officers and workmen. Were the boats sound? he would ask. How was the catch? Were the rapids high? His men worked faster when he appeared, stood very straight to talk with him, laughed at his jokes. But when things weren't right, he shouted in his "great voice" and brandished his cane.

Just as the day had a rhythm, so did the year. As the spring sun brightened, a fast overland express set

Grist mill of Fort Vancouver, built on a small stream running into the Columbia a few miles above the fort. It was the first water-powered mill in the area, forerunner of today's important industrial water power resources in the northwest.
OREGON HISTORICAL SOCIETY

out to carry letters upriver, across the Rockies on snowshoes, then by canoe, boat, and horseback to York Factory. It would return in the fall with the year's newspapers and mail.

In early June fur brigades swept up to the landing, having picked up boats and skins at every fort along the way. Although Dr. John rarely drank even wine, he opened a festival by taking a single glass. Everyone celebrated—visitors, seamen who had rounded the Horn, clerks and officers, some wearing fringed deerskins that had been gaily decorated by their Indian wives. Food and good fellowship were plentiful, but Dr. John didn't allow the heavy drinking and rioting of the old North West days at Fort William.

In autumn several fur brigades set out, the one to the Snake starting from Fort Walla Walla, those for the south leaving Fort Vancouver by boat, then changing to horses. The larger ones straggled in long lines with fifty to seventy-five men each, and hundreds of animals. Some went to the interior and spent the winter trapping and exploring, while others worked their way south and helped find a trail to California.

Most trappers took their wives to help with camp work, and Dr. John himself sometimes went along for

A Hudson's Bay Company fur brigade passing along the shore of a lake. Even on the trail the "gentleman" is wearing a beaver hat. Such brigades might include seventy-five men and hundreds of horses, stretching out for miles. NATIVE SONS OF BRITISH COLUMBIA

a day or so. Marguerite might go too, riding a fine horse with silver trappings and strings of bells. She beamed, on days like this, for women of the fort took their meals alone, saw few visitors, and had few outings.

Tough, eager, hard-working Dr. John traveled to many of his forts; upriver to the inland posts, downriver to Fort George, and overland to Puget's Sound. He was not only business manager and physician, he was judge and jury for the whole vast empire.

The year he built the new fort he made a far-reaching decision. A French Canadian trapper, Etienne Lucier, asked for help in settling in Wal-a-mot Valley. This was a parklike area south of the Columbia, where fir and oak groves stood between natural meadows that were spangled with flowers. A few retired free men lived there in an area called French Prairie. Knowing Lucier as "a good honest man," Dr. John lent him seed and wheat and sold him supplies at a low markup.

In the past, the company had required retirees to return to Canada for their discharge. "This was done to prevent vagabonds being let loose among the Indians and incite them to hostility to the whites," explained Dr. John. It would also keep settlers out of fur lands.

But he was troubled because men who were determined to settle in the west must make such a long trip, and he decided to help retirees, just as he had helped Lucier, provided they were good workers. To avoid paying a penalty, he kept them on the company books but gave them seed and wheat on credit, and later, when American trappers wanted to turn farmer, he extended the same terms to them.

In a few years a sturdy log cabin settlement was built on French Prairie. The wilderness was softening, for dark-eyed children played in the yards, fields of grain waved in place of blue-flowered camas, and rail fences zigzagged around kitchen gardens. McLoughlin provided two-wheeled carts, oxen, plows, household furniture, all to be paid for in wheat after raising a crop, and even though the fort didn't yet have many cows, he lent each settler two.

"If I sold a few cattle, only the rich could afford them," he said. "Since I only lent them, all had an equal chance."

When Governor Simpson found out about it, he ordered Dr. John to stop assisting the settlers, and reluctantly McLoughlin wrote, "Of course I will obey the order." Like it or not, he had no choice.

But he pointed out to the Committee that if he didn't help these men, many would still manage to begin farming, and would be resentful. Surely, he argued, it was better to aid the old servants and keep their friendship and raise a population which would help oppose future Yankee settlers.

"It Remains for your Honors to Decide," he said, and eventually the Governor and Committee acknowledged that his plan had been wiser than their own.

Although French Prairie didn't actually belong to the Hudson's Bay Company, the settlers brought crops and furs to the fort for sale, bought supplies there, and looked on Dr. John as their patron. He settled their disputes, gave them advice, and later, to save them the long trip to Fort Vancouver, he opened a branch ware-

Inside the palisade at Fort Vancouver, painted shortly after Dr. John left. The building on the right, with stairs to its veranda and cannon in front, is Dr. John's house. Its main

house and trading shop at a landing called Champoeg. One of them said, "The old doctor would go down to Champoeg, and whatever he told them to do, they would do . . . If there were any disputes, he settled them arbitrarily. Just what he said was the law."

Another said, "He was the finest man I ever knew,

floor was high off the ground, the space beneath being used for storage. HUDSON'S BAY COMPANY ARCHIVES, WINNIPEG

and there will never be another like him. He did what no other man would do."

Dr. John ruled an empire and found it so satisfying that he stopped writing about his wish to go down. At last he was truly a fur trader, a man of the West. Here he would build his career and his estate, here he would make his name.

The Columbia had become his home.

EIGHT

Dr. John's Dream

1829-1834

IN 1829, the year Dr. John built the new Fort Vancouver, an American ship *Owhyhee* dropped anchor in the Columbia. Friendly as always, McLoughlin pulled her off a sandbar, asked her Captain Dominis to dine at the fort, sent him lumber and potatoes. But business—that was different! Dr. John undersold him without mercy, and watched grimly as the price of a blanket plummeted from five beaver to one, a gun from eighteen to six. No matter what, he was determined to drive off the Yankee, and he wrote to London, "It would be adviseable to give Indns. even two Blankets for a large Beaver . . . as even at this rate the price at which Beaver sell in England will leave us a profit."

Dominis finally left with a load of skins, and Dr.

John gradually restored the old prices. But this Yankee ship had paid havoc with his trade. Somehow he had to keep the "Bostons" (Chinook jargon for Americans) from making money on the coast. Then they would stay away.

Dr. John had a dream—to build forts in the far north, establish trade with the Russians, and drive out the American ships. He wanted a whole chain of forts, so many that whenever a Yankee coaster came along, the nearest Hudson's Bay post could send out a vessel to anchor near the Boston and undersell him. Simpson didn't agree, for he preferred a strong fleet. But Dr. John pointed out his troubles with ships and their captains, and insisted, "I can maintain four posts for the cost of one vessel."

However, he couldn't realize his dream right then because an epidemic began of "intermittent fever"—malaria. It was serious for the whites, but worse for Indians, who had no resistance to it and treated it by plunging into the frigid Columbia. In one village all died except one boy who, being a slave, had been left without the "treatment"—the icy dip. One trader reported:

". . . the living sufficed not to bury their dead, but fled in terror to the seacoast, abandoning the dead and dying to the birds and beasts of prey. Every village presented a scene harrowing to the feelings; the canoes were there drawn up upon the beach, the nets extended on the willow-boughs to dry, the very dogs appeared as ever, watchful, but there was not the cheerful sound of the human voice."

Dr. John was swamped. Having no quinine, he used dogwood roots instead. He couldn't persuade the Indians to give up their chilling baths. Fifty of his men were sick. He had to have the furs beaten weekly for moths, attend to the farm and shops, see that all his posts had supplies. Many natives flocked to the fort and camped just outside the palisade, hoping for treatment and knowing that if they died, the King George Men would bury them.

One bright spot that troubled year was the arrival of James Douglas, twenty-seven, and so well-mannered that some people laughed at his "grand airs." But he was able and sincere, a good man to have as assistant and bookkeeper.

Dr. John needed him, for the next summer the plague returned. "From daylight until eleven at night" he was busy visiting the sick and trying to operate the fort, short-handed. He was weary. To make things worse, a large canoe upset in a rapids at the Dalles, drowning nine, and within a few weeks seven more were drowned farther upriver.

"I say I was employed but in truth I might say harrassed in mind and Body as much as possibly could be," he wrote.

James Douglas, for many years Dr. John's right-hand man. When Fort Vancouver was abandoned, Douglas served as chief of the new headquarters at Fort Victoria and became the first governor of the Vancouver Island and British Columbia colonies of Canada. PROVINCIAL ARCHIVES, VICTORIA, B.C.

Fall, even with its rain, was welcome, for the disease subsided, and the Governor and Committee at last sent a two-year supply of trading goods, which meant that from now on he would receive outfits a year in advance. He wrote in relief, "This is the first year since I am here . . . in which I have been able to supply our people adequately." He also thankfully received control of all shipping and captains.

Summer after summer the disease returned. Dr. John trained a young clerk to help treat it, fortunately, for he himself fell sick. He received some quinine, which worked better and was more convenient than dogwood roots, but the fort had hardly enough able-bodied men to do the work.

Even though the fever was still on the rampage, Dr. John didn't forget his dream. Before the disease struck, he had put up Fort Langley, and in 1831 he managed to build Fort Simpson farther north.

The next summer he sent out three small craft, commanded by Peter Skene Ogden, who had formerly led the Snake brigade.

"Underbid the Americans," Dr. John instructed Ogden, so the trader followed the coasters from inlet to inlet, offering twice as much as the Bostons—three times as much. They played a kind of watery tag. Every time a Hudson's Bay vessel appeared, the American would slip away, with the British ship in hot pursuit. But the Yankees still collected most of the furs because they traded in liquor, which Dr. John's men scorned to do.

Finally Ogden too offered "spirits." Dr. John re-

Peter Skene Ogden, an important Hudson's Bay officer. Short, dark, very tough, with an inexhaustible sense of humor, Ogden was popular at the fort and a special friend to Dr. John. He moved to Oregon City soon after McLoughlin did and lived there until his death in 1854. OREGON HISTORICAL SOCIETY

luctantly agreed, and Simpson himself said the company must either do so or "abandon the contest altogether."

The following year, 1833, the last year of severe plague, McLoughlin managed to have two more forts built, Nisqually near Puget Sound, and one named for himself, McLoughlin, farther north. Winter came, a sad winter, with the Indian villages all but lifeless, for ninety percent of the Columbia tribes had perished. Gray mist hung over the river and rain veiled the opposite shore.

All through the plague years Dr. John had carried a heavy load as physician and also as director of the entire Columbia district plus his own fort. However, he had received no more pay than any other chief factor. Realizing this, the Governor and Committee voted him a bonus of eleven hundred pounds, which he well deserved.

And now, with the illness over, he could try again for a foothold in the north.

Behind the narrow coastal strip of Russian Alaska lay an enormous sweep of fur land that was in joint occupancy, and therefore open to the British. A treaty with Russia said they could cross the strip to reach those

Dr. John's empire, showing the border of Mexico before 1848 and that of Russia before the United States bought Alaska. All the land west of the Rocky Mountains and between Russia and Mexico was in joint occupancy. Besides the important posts shown here, McLoughlin supervised many small ones in the interior.

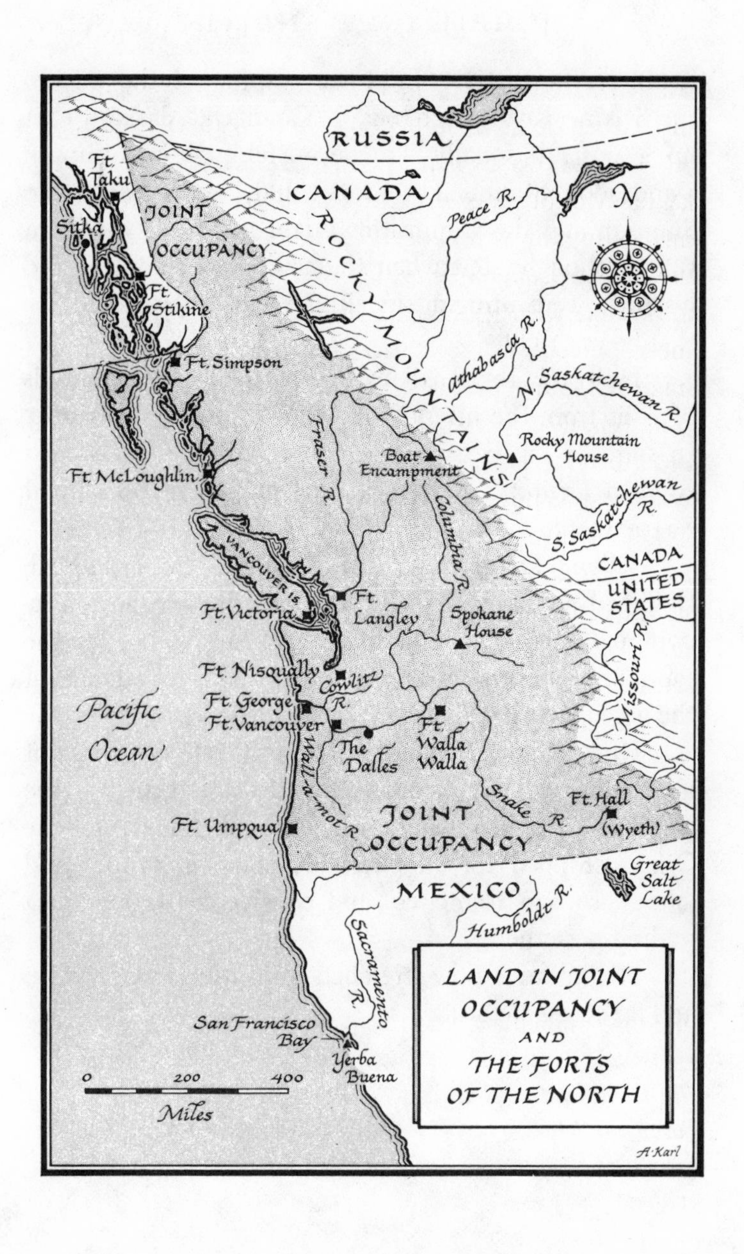
RUSSIA
CANADA
ROCKY MOUNTAINS
Peace R.
N
Ft. Taku
JOINT OCCUPANCY
Sitka
Ft. Stikine
Ft. Simpson
Athabasca R.
N. Saskatchewan R.
Fraser R.
Boat Encampment
Rocky Mountain House
Ft. McLoughlin
S. Saskatchewan R.
Columbia R.
Vancouver Is.
CANADA
UNITED STATES
Ft. Langley
Ft. Victoria
Spokane House
Missouri R.
Ft. Nisqually
Cowlitz R.
Ft. George
Ft. Vancouver
Pacific Ocean
The Dalles
Ft. Walla Walla
Wall-a-mot R.
Snake R.
Ft. Hall (Wyeth)
JOINT OCCUPANCY
Ft. Umpqua
Great Salt Lake
MEXICO
Humboldt R.
Sacramento R.
San Francisco Bay
Yerba Buena
0 200 400
Miles
LAND IN JOINT OCCUPANCY AND THE FORTS OF THE NORTH
A·Karl

lands, so in 1834 Dr. John sent Ogden all the way to the Stikine River, near today's Wrangell, Alaska, to set up a post. Nisqually–Langley–McLoughlin–Simpson –and soon Stikine. Dr. John could count them over. Simpson and the Committee might not agree with him yet, he thought, but when the chain was complete and his forts were bringing in all the furs, they would see that he was right.

However, the Russians had been buying thousands of skins from the interior, and they didn't want to stop. In spite of the treaty, they refused to let Ogden cross Russian territory, and threatened to fire on his ship if he tried force.

When Dr. John heard about it, he grumbled, thumped his cane, and sat down to write a disgusted report to London. He couldn't afford to give up, for the southern furs were nearly gone, and the rich lands of the north were his only hope for a decent profit.

He was also looking in other directions, and not for furs alone. His company founded an agency in the Sandwich Islands, where whalers and traders to the Orient stopped for supplies. He shipped lumber and salmon to San Francisco, and considered setting up a trading post there.

His interests now stretched from Mexico to Alaska, and far across the sea.

NINE

End of Isolation
1832-1838

AS the fever subsided, more Americans crossed the mountains and came to the Columbia. Dr. John welcomed them in his hearty voice and freely showed his dairy, croplands, "piggery," fields extending fifteen miles along the river and five miles inland. If they wanted to visit Wal-a-mot Valley, he supplied boats and voyageurs and "all the necessaries of the voyage." Liking companionship, liking men of ideas, he was genuinely glad to see them—most of them.

One visitor, William Slacum, was a spy sent by the American government. Although Slacum pretended to be only sightseeing, Dr. John wrote, "This did not deceive me, as I perceived who he was and his object." Nevertheless, he entertained the Yankee at the fort for two weeks, then lent him a canoe and voyageurs for a visit to Wal-a-mot Valley.

In spite of the kindness shown him, Slacum carried back a cruelly unfair report. It spoke of the "thraldom" of the Hudson's Bay Company," called it an "immense foreign monopoly," and accused it, falsely, of keeping slaves and mistreating Indians. But most of Dr. John's guests spread glowing accounts of the lush prairies and forests, the bustling fort, and its kind-hearted chief factor. All over the United States, people were growing interested in the west coast.

Another important visitor was Nathaniel J. Wyeth from Boston, a big, handsome, bearded ice merchant who had traveled overland but sent a ship of trading goods around the Horn. He and his young followers remained all winter at Fort Vancouver "eating and drinking the good things to be had there and enjoying much the gentlemanly society of the place."

Dr. John, with his lively interest in science and ideas, had fostered an amazing atmosphere for a wilderness outpost. He had eagerly welcomed and assisted several visiting botanists and biologists, such as David Douglas, and had sent specimens and data to London. The "gentlemen's hall" housed an exhibit of animals and Indian artifacts. He encouraged one of Wyeth's men to start the first school in the northwest, for the children of the fort, and encouraged the first lending library, its books kept in a large desk. He also had an interest in history, Napoleon being one of his favorite characters. Conversation at the fort was good. Small wonder Wyeth enjoyed it.

Nathaniel J. Wyeth, the Boston ice merchant who tried to found a business on the Columbia. Even though Wyeth caused the first rift between Dr. John and the Hudson's Bay Company, the two remained friends. Late in his life Wyeth gave Dr. John a twelve-volume biography of Napoleon, and when McLoughlin's enemies asked him to write a critical letter, the staunch Yankee refused. OREGON HISTORICAL SOCIETY

By spring, realizing his ship was lost, the Yankee made ready to leave. "I parted with feelings of sorrow from the gentlemen of Fort Vancouver," he wrote. He spoke of Dr. John's "kindness and humanity," his "good sense and information," and said "he will never be forgotten by me."

Within a few months Wyeth returned, this time offering Dr. John a deal. If the Hudson's Bay men would not interfere with his fishing and horse trading, he would not trap or trade any furs except farther east. To Dr. John this seemed like good sense, because it would not be costly, and he was sure the flimsy venture would fail of its own accord. Besides, he liked the Yankee and didn't want on open conflict. So he consulted with the other gentlemen, then agreed.

As he expected, Wyeth had nothing but trouble. His nets weren't right. His men couldn't catch fish. Fourteen drowned or were killed. After two years he gave up and left, returning once more to sell out to the British.

But the Governor and Committee weren't satisfied. They insisted that any kind of cooperation might encourage other Americans to come, and that it would have been better to oppose Wyeth "vigorously."

This outraged Dr. John's prickly sense of justice, for his plan had worked so well that he had "thwarted" the competition without spending a farthing, and without "the shadow of an angry word." Since he was responsible for the area, he thought the Committee should back his judgment. He brooded, couldn't overlook it.

Fuming, he asked the gentlemen of the fort to confirm his handling of the problem and packed their replies off to London, and a year later he sent off another batch. Even though Dr. John and Wyeth remained lifelong friends, the Yankee had innocently caused the first rift between McLoughlin and the London officers.

About that same time some other Americans arrived who were going to have a lasting impact on the area and on Dr. John's life. They were five Methodist missionaries who had traveled with Wyeth partway and were following him down the Columbia in Hudson's Bay boats. Dr. John was delighted. For many years he had read the Bible on Sundays, in English for the gentlemen and in French for the Catholic Canadians. He had asked the company to send a minister of the Church of England and petitioned the bishop at Red River for priests. Now at last men of God had come.

As soon as messengers told him they were near, Dr. John hurried down to the landing. White hair gleaming, he raised his cane in greeting, helped them ashore, and as he walked with them up the long path to the fort, he was full of eager questions and offers of help.

Their leader was Jason Lee, almost as tall as Dr. John, slow-moving and a little stooped, but loyal and truthful and afire with eagerness to save the Indians' souls. Dr. John saw that they were fed and had his men put their baggage into their rooms. Besides housing them for several weeks at the fort, he gave them animals and supplies and lent them boats and voyageurs to search for an ideal site. They decided on a low-lying place on the east side of the Wal-a-mot River, about thirty miles south of Fort Vancouver and called it Mission Bottoms.

McLoughlin welcoming the Whitman party on the dock of Fort Vancouver. Dr. John reaches toward Narcissa and James Douglas greets Eliza Spalding, while Marcus Whitman, in beaver hat, and the Reverend Spalding, holding his, wait.

After two years, more missionaries, including a few women, came to help Lee, and again Dr. John aided them. Weak as it was and plagued with problems, this mission marked a watershed. Earlier Americans had come only to leave again, but from the time Lee arrived they would always be present. Although Dr. John welcomed them, he must have realized that their mission was growing and some day would challenge him for control of the Columbia. But he couldn't have guessed the final tragedy.

Clerks, trappers and laborers always turned out for the arrival of visitors. From a mural in the Oregon State Capitol building.
OREGON STATE HIGHWAY DEPARTMENT

Other churches were also interested in the west. Shortly before Lee's second group arrived, Dr. Marcus Whitman and the Reverend H. H. Spalding appeared, along with their wives, the first white women to cross overland. Dr. John housed them at the fort while their husbands built missions in the dry sagebrush hills of the interior.

Narcissa Whitman called Fort Vancouver "the New York of the Pacific," noted that French was the language there and said Marguerite was "one of the kindest women in the world." She wrote in her journal, "Doct McLaughlin gave my Husband a pair of Lether pantaloons today. all the gentlemen here were them for economy. Riding horseback & carrying a gun is very destructive to cloth pantaloons."

When they left, Dr. John gave them farm tools, coffee and tea pots, candlesticks and molds, pails and an oven. He, or perhaps Marguerite, also delighted Narcissa by giving her a "fether bed."

That same year, 1836, the Governor and Committee sent out a minister of a different stripe, from Dr. John's own Church of England. He was a short stout man with a high-pitched voice and fondness for long sermons. The only thing about him that suited the fur trade was his name, Herbert Beaver.

Nothing at Fort Vancouver pleased him or his wife. For a few months they lived in a part-dwelling which they called a "personal insult and domestic annoyance." The attic over their quarters was used by workmen who went there "regardless of Mrs. Beaver's convenience." Even when Dr. John gave them the best separate house he had, they weren't content, for it had a mud and stone chimney in the center and only two rooms—dining-room-kitchen; bedroom-parlor. On the floor were rush mats "too filthy to step upon," and the Beavers were indignant when McLoughlin refused to recommend carpets as not suited to a fort.

The Reverend Beaver taught a school at Fort Vancouver, but it failed because he tried to force Episcopal beliefs on French Canadian children.

He and Dr. John had trouble over wine, because

McLoughlin thought it should be served only at dinner, but Beaver always offered it to his guests, and drew more than his allotment.

Conducting three full—and very long—services every Sunday, he called the mess hall, the only large meeting room, "an indecent place too small to hold all the Sunday School children" and objected because some families living in the same building "do not attend me." He was indignant because McLoughlin held services for his Catholic workmen, and because Catholics used the same room as his own flock.

In reply Dr. John ironically reported, "I cannot perceive the impropriety of assembling our English and Canadian servants for public worship in the same appartment or by the sound of the same Bell."

Worst of all, the Reverend was disgusted because the gentlemen hadn't been formally married. He said they were "living in sin," although he didn't explain what they could have arranged in the wilderness, with neither church nor court for thousands of miles.

The officers tried to pacify him. James Douglas and his young wife Amelia were remarried, and Eloisa became the bride of a promising young Hudson's Bay clerk named William Glen Rae, with the Reverend Beaver in charge. Dr. John legally remarried Marguerite, although he drew the line at having the ceremony performed by the Reverend Beaver. Instead he called in his friend James Douglas, newly appointed justice of the peace.

Nothing helped. The cleric pestered Dr. John with letter after letter. He tried to go over Dr. John's head by sending complaints direct to Governor Simpson, but

The only surviving picture of Marguerite, taken late in her life after she had grown quite stout. Dr. John always honored her and insisted that employees stand and remove their hats in her presence. OREGON HISTORICAL SOCIETY

the governor returned them with orders to send them through the proper channel—McLoughlin.

Dr. John had to read them as part of his job. Cantankerous as they were, he let them pass until one called Marguerite "a female of notoriously loose character" and "the kept mistress of the highest personage in your service at this station."

This was too much. Meeting the Reverend crossing the yard, Dr. John demanded an explanation.

"Sire," replied Beaver. "If you wish to know why

a cow's tail grows downward I cannot tell you; I can only cite the fact."

Dr. John exploded. He kicked the minister, struck him on the neck, seized his walking stick and pounded him with it, grabbed him by the waist and tried to throw him. "You scoundrel, I will have your life!" he roared.

Mrs. Beaver had been watching with understandable interest. When McLoughlin dropped the stick, she picked it up. He snatched it back. She screeched. The Reverend called for his pistols. And in the end, bystanders separated them.

As always, Dr. John's anger quickly cooled. The next day at an auction in the public square, he stood up in front of the crowd. "Mr. Beaver, I—I make this public apology for the indignity I laid upon you yesterday," he said.

"Sire, I will not accept your apology!" was the stiff reply.

They never patched up the quarrel. Later on, when James Douglas had temporary charge of the fort, he and Beaver started on a friendly basis, but before long the Reverend was so disagreeable that Douglas refused to have anything to do with him. At last, to everyone's relief, the Beavers packed up and went back to England.

Meanwhile the Yankees continued to move in, and at Fort Vancouver during the long winter evenings in Bachelors' Hall, the gentlemen talked heatedly about them. Loving a good argument, Dr. John stoutly defended the newcomers.

"They have the same right to come that I have to be here," he often said.

When company retirees worried about moving to French Prairie, where Americans would be their neighbors, he assured them, "The American Government and people know only two classes of persons, rogues and honest men; they punish the first and protect the last, and it depends only upon yourself to what class you belong."

But the Americans he defended—those who stayed and those who left—were changing Dr. John's world.

TEN

Zenith
1838-1841

IT was fourteen years since Dr. John had gone to a summer gathering, and nine since he had seen Governor Simpson. Although he had several times planned a furlough, something had always interfered, but now the Committee in London wanted a personal report on Ogden's trouble entering the Stikine River.

Dr. John's children were established—Joe farming nearby, Elizabeth married and living in the east, Eloisa also happily married, and David just finishing school in England. Even young John, a hot-tempered, turbulent boy who had worried all the relatives with his many scrapes, had settled down and joined the company as apprentice clerk. With the family and trade both prospering, it was a good time for McLoughlin to leave. So on March 22, 1838, he proudly took his seat in a bateau and watched his son John also climb in, to go partway.

The trip was strenuous. "It is no joke to cross the Mountains in the Spring Snow eleven [feet] deep," young John wrote to a cousin.

In the East, McLoughlin booked passage in the famous *Great Western,* the first steamship built for the Atlantic trade, and when he reached Europe he had two Davids to visit—his brother in Paris, and his son in England.

This time in London was very different from Dr. John's first, when he represented the wintering partners and had little status. Now, honored and consulted, he took a hand in two important changes.

First, his company secured a ten-year lease of the narrow, southern finger of Alaska, which meant he could move at last toward completing his chain of forts.

Second, since they were to supply the Russians wheat, peas, grits, hulled pot barley, salted beef, butter and pork, the Committee set up a new Puget Sound Agricultural Company. Dr. John had suggested this several years before, but Governor Simpson had scornfully opposed it. Now McLoughlin not only had won out, he would be superintendent and receive an extra five hundred pounds per year.

The journey back was a triumphal procession. Young David was with him, for he had somehow persuaded—or required—the boy to come along. At Montreal Dr. John helped Governor Simpson make plans for accepting the Russian land lease. At Red River he was named to a special group that advised Simpson and got David ap-

Nisqually, on Puget Sound, painted in the 1840s by Paul Kane. This important post was a farm, the heart of the Puget Sound Agriculture Company, and also a shipping center. Expeditions to the north could go overland from Fort Vancouver to Nisqually, and there transfer to a ship.
STARK MUSEUM OF ART, ORANGE, TEXAS

pointed as apprentice clerk. At Lake Winnipeg he met young John, then started home with both sons, crossed the mountains, and scudded down the Columbia in two boats, using Indian blankets as sails, and arriving on October 17, 1839. Marguerite could rejoice, for her men had all safely returned. The clerks and laborers rejoiced too. James Douglas was efficient and courteous—but genial, warm-hearted, quick-tempered Dr. John was the one they loved.

He was proud as his strapping young sons settled into work at the fort. "I must say that they are as attentive and smart at their work as most young men," he wrote.

However, they weren't together long. Only a few months later, on April 26, 1840, he parted with sadness, yet with pride, from his daughter Eloisa and her young husband, William Glen Rae, and from his son John. They were going to the far north and take over the Russian post on the Stikine River that Ogden had been barred from entering. There Rae was to command the fort, with John his first assistant.

Huddled on a barren point of land scarcely large enough to hold the buildings, at high tide Fort Stikine was an island, but when the ocean receded, it left a rocky isthmus covered with stinking green slime. Because it had no wells, water was brought in by a wooden trough which the natives frequently destroyed.

"It was a miserable place," said Eloisa. "There were only flat rocks and not trees around close. Within half a mile, just bare rocks."

The Russians had ruled by brute force, which made the Stikine Indians hate all whites, and both Russians and Americans had traded in liquor. Possibly, in making his plans, Dr. John had underestimated the danger. The Russian officer in command of fifty men was horrified to find that they meant to leave only William Glen Rae, young John McLoughlin, and eighteen others there.

"It's unsafe," the Russians insisted.

"Other forts we rule with twenty men and we will hold Stikine," the British replied.

Unfortunately, Dr. John had been so short of men

Medicine Man Mask Dance, painted in the 1840s by Paul Kane. These are Indians of the far north, where Fort Stikine and several others were located. The masks were of wood, beautifully carved and painted. Later, after they acquired metal knives, the Indians of the northwest carved totem poles.
ROYAL ONTARIO MUSEUM

that most of these eighteen were the roughest, most unruly characters in the entire company. He was counting on Rae and young John to keep them in line.

In a few days the *Beaver* pushed on north to plant Fort Taku, near today's Juneau, almost fulfilling Dr. John's dream. He could list them with pride—Nisqually, Langley, Simpson, McLoughlin, Stikine and Taku. One more, on Vancouver Island, would do the job.

Besides the new forts, Dr. John had been ordered

Yerba Buena, now downtown San Francisco. The large building on Montgomery Street, to the left of Clay, is the Hudson's Bay Company property, which was a combination house and store when William Glen Rae and Eloisa lived

there. Eloisa was active in the social life of California. Its governor, General Vallejo, lived in the house numbered 27.
HUDSON'S BAY COMPANY

to open a trading post at Yerba Buena on San Francisco Bay. Being short of men, within a few months he transferred Eloisa's husband, William Glen Rae, from Stikine to California, and appointed young John in Rae's place. This wasn't through favoritism, but because John had earned it by serving the company well. Even though most of the men at Stikine were ruffians, McLoughlin's son had one competent aide, Roderick Finlayson.

In the spring of 1841, when Rae set out for California, Dr. John could feel well pleased, with both these exciting new posts well launched. But two of his family were in peril. Eloisa's husband was bound for a foreign country that was full of intrigue. Young John was at lawless Fort Stikine, surrounded by hostile natives, with only one trustworthy aide and a treacherous crew.

The stage was set.

ELEVEN

The Winds of Change

1840-1841

IN late May, 1840, a single canoe pulled up to Fort Vancouver and a tall, stoop-shouldered, bearded man jumped out. It was Dr. John's old friend, the Reverend Jason Lee, who had gone East soon after McLoughlin left for London. Lee had made scores of speeches and raised $42,000 plus a large group of recruits, both men and women. This was the "Great Reinforcement," brought around the Horn. While the ship crept up the Columbia, he had hurried ahead to alert the fort.

At once Dr. John began to issue orders, preparing to house all these guests. Ten days later, when the ship finally dropped anchor, he went aboard, greeted everyone in his hearty voice, and invited the leaders to tea.

Jason Lee, leader of the first group of Methodist missionaries and founder of the missions at Mission Bottoms and Chemeketa. Although he couldn't control the land-hunger of some of his followers, Lee himself was Dr. John's friend.
OREGON HISTORICAL SOCIETY

By the time the whole company moved into the fort, it hummed with missionaries. Those from Mission Bottoms paddled upriver to greet the newcomers and admire their fashionable city clothes, and one couple was married in Dr. John's own home.

With this Great Reinforcement the whole thrust of the mission changed. Lee and his first group had truly wanted to help the Indians, but most of these new missionaries dreamed of a rich, powerful colony that would control the entire area. Even though Jason Lee had warned the church board in the east that they weren't being careful enough in accepting recruits, the board hadn't listened.

Lee was brimming with plans. He meant to abandon Mission Bottoms and build a new headquarters at Chemeketa, a grassy spot farther upriver, which the missionaries renamed Salem.

He assigned his new aides to posts all over the area sending Reverend Alvin H. Waller to the falls of the Willamette, the falls Dr. John and Governor Simpson had claimed in 1829. Dr. John had improved the site by having his men blast out a mill race and put up a rough building. Although as yet he had no way to register a land claim, he meant to hold it for his company if he could, otherwise for himself.

Within a few weeks Lee asked him to let the Reverend Waller use some squared timbers that still lay there. "To build the mission," Lee explained, and added that one end would be a small store.

While Dr. John might easily have said he needed it and that plenty of other timber stood nearby for the cutting, that wasn't his way. He not only let Waller use the lumber, he also let him put the building on his own grounds. It was a mistake. Waller quickly realized the value of the falls and decided to get it.

Soon McLoughlin heard that the missionaries were

planning to jump his claim. Impossible, he thought. Not Jason Lee, that shambling young giant he had so often befriended. He wrote Lee a stout letter of protest.

"I beg to inform you that in 1830 as is well known to most of the old settlers in the Wallamette I took possession of the side of the Falls . . . which I intend to claim when the Boundary line is drawn."

But his anger quickly cooled, and he added a friendly postscript. "Of course this is not to prevent your building the store, as my object is merely to establish my claim."

Although Lee first replied that the missionaries didn't intend to dispute McLoughlin's title, he later said he couldn't "controul any man." Dr. John was puzzled. The area might become American, and United States law allowed only individuals, not companies, to claim land. How could he protect his property when nobody knew which country's laws to follow? To be on the safe side, he opened a mill of his own, while Waller put up a house and moved into it—a house built of Dr. John's timber, on Dr. John's land.

The valley of the Willamette River was the heart of early settlement. Wall-a-mot Falls became Oregon City, Dr. John's home; and Chemeketa became Salem, the present state capital. Champoeg was the staging area for fur brigades to the south. Supplies were sent to it by the long route up the Wall-a-mot River while pack trains went overland by the Hudson's Bay Company trail.

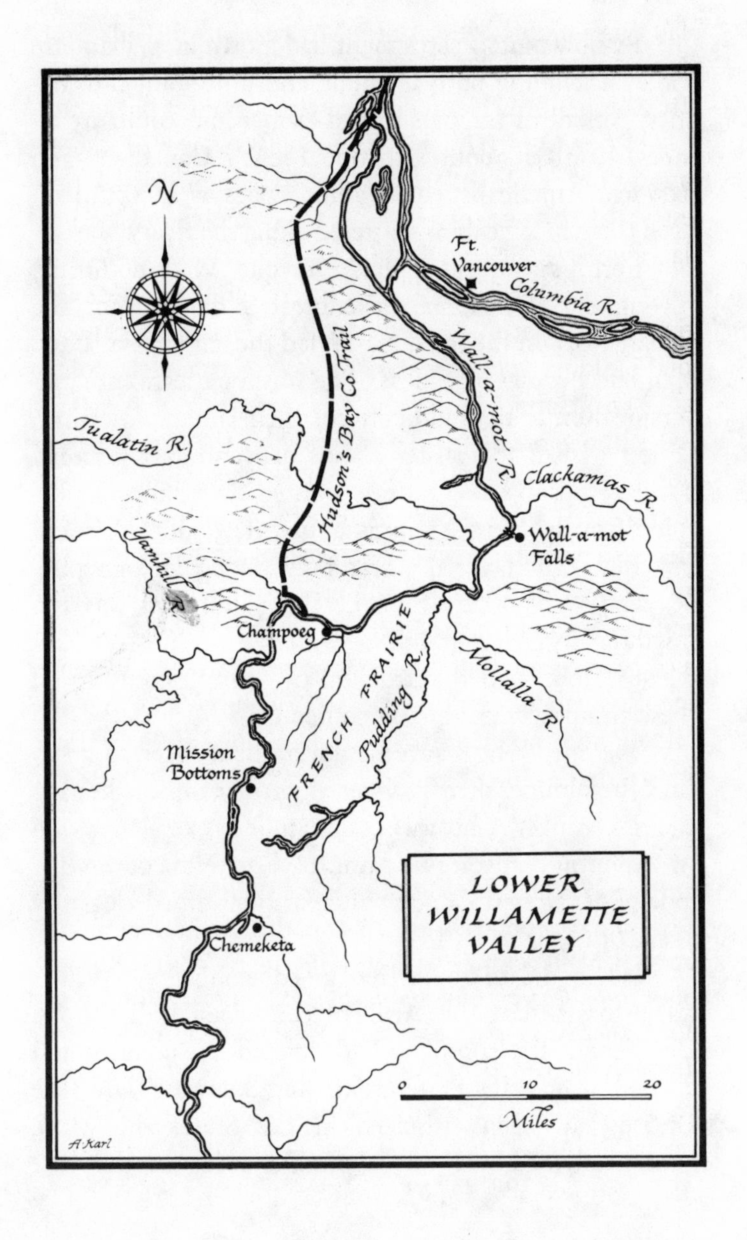
N
Ft. Vancouver
Columbia R.
Hudson's Bay Co. Trail
Wall-a-mot R.
Tualatin R.
Clackamas R.
Wall-a-mot Falls
Yamhill R.
Champoeg
FRENCH PRAIRIE
Pudding R.
Mollalla R.
Mission Bottoms
Chemeketa
LOWER WILLAMETTE VALLEY
0
10
20
Miles
A Karl

By now quite a settlement had grown in Willamette Valley, including both Catholic and protestant missionaries, American trappers-turned-farmer and company retirees. In 1841 about sixty-one French Canadians and sixty-five Americans (only adult males were counted) lived there in log cabins scattered along the rivers.

Fort Vancouver supplied everyone. With no formal government, Dr. John was almost a dictator for the Canadians, and the missionaries led the Americans. Each man had his own pet ideas. The missionaries wanted an organization that would confirm their large land claims. Others wished to register claims or were after personal power. Hudson's Bay retirees wanted the country to become British. Most Yankees hoped it would be American. But many favored a brand-new independent republic, while still others thought the population was too small for any government.

Dr. John had the problem of being friendly to all these groups, yet loyal to his company.

The men who wanted a government received a setback the summer of 1841 when the American Lieutenant Charles Wilkes, who was commanding several ships on an exploring expedition, came to Fort Vancouver. He rode with the beribboned voyageurs and dined elegantly at the fort.

Having heard about the "greedy company," Wilkes was astonished at the excellent care given Indian boys. He thought the company had quieted the country and opened it to safe emigration, and knowing how the British had been criticized in the States, he wrote sarcastically, "There was abundant evidence that the odious monopoly was at least as generous as any octopus of commerce could afford to be."

Since the lieutenant wanted to see the Valley, Dr. John sent him south in a large boat. Some of the settlers asked Wilkes for advice about forming a government, but instead of encouraging them, he urged them to wait. Privately he said their principal reasons were to "induce settlers to flock in, thereby raising the value of their farms and stock."

After a few weeks the friendly American left for the States with a report which praised the Hudson's Bay men, especially Dr. John. More important, Wilkes had dampened down the new missionaries' push for control.

But that was only for the time being. The winds of change were blowing.

TWELVE

The Quarrel Begins

1841-1842

ON August 25, 1841, paddle songs were heard and a special flotilla swept up to the dock. In it was Governor Simpson—Sir George Simpson now, having been recently knighted—on his way around the world. Although he was almost blind and could write only through a secretary, he was energetic as ever, traveling fast, making plans and changes, accompanied by "a dashing train." After a brief stay he left with James Douglas to inspect the northern forts.

At Stikine Sir George found that even without William Glen Rae young John McLoughlin had affairs well in hand, had packed the furs properly, and repaired the palisade. Concluding that the young man could manage alone, Sir George transferred the only trustworthy assistant to another fort.

It worried young John. "I am sorry to say that Mr. Finlayson is taken away," he wrote to another officer.

Sir George Simpson, for many years Governor-in-Chief of all the territories of the Hudson's Bay Company in America. The quarrel with Simpson marked the turning point of Dr. John's career. HUDSON'S BAY COMPANY

The Beaver, *first steamship on the coast, surrounded by dugout canoes, in harbor at Port Simpson, which is not far from Stikine. Dr. John's dislike for the* Beaver *intensified his*

quarrel with Simpson. She was not very efficient and after one day's run she had to stop while six men chopped wood for two days to refill her bins. NATIONAL MUSEUM OF CANADA

"The one McPherson that is left in his place will never answer the purpose."

He implored the heads of nearby forts to send trustworthy help, watched daily for the steamer, and decided not to renew his contract unless he received a competent aide. Fort Stikine was surrounded by hostile natives and manned by what could only be called a gang. The men resented young John's discipline, and he knew it.

"I am still amongst the living of this troublesome post, though reports says that I am going to be dispatched to the *Sandy Hills*," he said. "I cannot trust to no one . . . I do not know what to do in the evening when I cannot sleep."

By late October Simpson returned to Fort Vancouver and announced Finlayson's transfer. Although Dr. John was anxious, Sir George assured him that he had confidence in the young man, and "all would be well." He then dropped a bomb. He was going to close most of the northern posts and use ships instead, relying especially on the *Beaver*, first steamship on the coast.

This was a shock, for Dr. John had just opened some of those forts at terrible cost. They were dependable, he thought, while ships were always out of repair. Vessels came and went, but any time the natives had goods to trade, the post was there. He especially detested the *Beaver*, which he considered expensive and hard to keep in repair.

Moreover, Simpson had worked out the plan without consulting McLoughlin, which seemed to reflect on his management. After all his years of hard work, it hurt. In his disappointment, "unable to think of anything else," Dr. John almost forgot about young John alone at Fort Stikine, and James Douglas bluntly told the governor, ". . . the slashing paragraphs in your report, denouncing abuses on shore and afloat gave him inexpressible pain."

Sir George stood firm. He insisted that because of the new treaty with the Russian American Company, permanent posts were not needed, and that the plan would save four thousand pounds per year.

He also decided to move headquarters to a new Fort on Vancouver Island, in Puget Sound. He had good reasons which he spelled out. The bar at the mouth of the Columbia was dangerous. A post farther north would be more central. The boundary decision might give Fort Vancouver to America. Yankees, moving in, might plunder a wealthy fort.

When the Governor and Committee had talked before about moving headquarters, Dr. John had argued that they must remain strong on the Columbia. Besides, building Fort Vancouver had been his life's great work. He knew every shop, every employee, had watched nearly every building rise. But no matter how he fumed and protested, Simpson stood his ground.

With the dispute still burning, the two left in January, 1842, for California. There, although Sir George kept silent, he was displeased with William Glen Rae's post at Yerba Buena.

When they sailed for the Sandwich Islands, McLoughlin was still determined not to give up. Not without a struggle. On the tossing ship he sat day after day,

Crossing the bar at the entrance of the Columbia River. The William and Ann *was wrecked here, as were others. Often a ship couldn't cross for days or weeks, but must wait until the wind and tide were right. This was one reason Simpson wanted to move headquarters farther north.* OREGON HISTORICAL SOCIETY

big frame bent forward, writing a long report and pages of figures to defend his hard-won forts. He might as well not have bothered, for Simpson was resolved to cut them out: to use ships; to move headquarters. He was brooding about Rae's post, and one day he abruptly said he had decided to close it entirely. Although downtown San Francisco was eventually built there, Simpson called it "a wretched place," and "not fit for an establishment."

"You exceeded orders in starting it when you did," he snapped.

"I followed the London agreements to the letter," Dr. John replied.

"It isn't paying."

"It will surely prove profitable in time."

Sir George had charge of the company in America. Dr. John was director on the Columbia. Both were used to running their own shows, both were stubborn and proud, and neither would give in. For seventeen years they had been on friendly terms, exchanging letters and making plans together. Simpson had visited the McLoughlin children when they were in school in the east, and had tried to help young John through some of his schoolboy scrapes. But now friendship was forgotten. Angrily deciding to get their views on record, while they were at "Wahoo" (Oahu) they wrote each other a series of bitter reports.

Of course, Sir George, the superior officer, won. He gave Dr. John firm instructions to abandon Forts Taku and McLoughlin, to close Yerba Buena, and to build a new headquarters on Vancouver Island. Humiliated, furious, McLoughlin accused Simpson of not permitting a fair discussion because his mind was made up before he came to the coast.

Still smarting from the quarrel, he returned to the Columbia and tried to take up the reins at Fort Vancouver, while Simpson again went north.

THIRTEEN

What Happened on the Stikine

1842

THE next June when the company ship came back, she brought two horrifying letters from Simpson. One said that on reaching Stikine he found the Russian and British flags at half mast and everything silent. Only one man appeared at the gate, "evidently showing that there was a mournful tale to relate, and on landing, I was more shocked than words can describe to learn that Mr. McLoughlin was no more, having fallen . . . in a drunken Fray, by the hand of one of his own men."

Dr. John was stunned. His son—who was doing so well—murdered! Never to return from the dark forests of the north!

This long letter contained not one word of sympathy

for a sorrowing father. It called John's conduct and management "exceedingly bad," said that when he drank he showed violence "amounting to insanity," and that the act was done "under the influence of terror, as a measure of self preservation . . . my belief is, that any Tribunal by which the case could be tried, would find a verdict of 'Justifiable Homicide.' "

Sir George enclosed statements by the men, who said one of their number had shot John in self-defense, because of his cruelty. He called the men's conduct "better than could have been expected under such inhuman treatment, as they were frequently exposed to . . . The accounts, I fear are in a very irregular state."

Only one sentence of the other letter survives, but it was apparently a personal note advising Dr. John not to press charges.

On his first visit to Stikine Sir George had been well impressed, had called McLoughlin's son "one of the smartest young men in the country," and had found everything in good order. But he also knew of the schoolboy scrapes, and perhaps the quarrel with Dr. John still rankled. So he made only a hasty inquiry, picked up the man who had fired the fatal shot, turned him over to Russian authorities and wrote the cruel letters.

McLoughlin read them, and read them again—with grief—with rage. If Simpson meant the murderer was not to be prosecuted—never—never would he accept that! He'd see that justice was done. He'd find out the truth. Sir George had left his son alone in that perilous spot. But for him, young John would still be alive.

Distraught as he was, Dr. John tried to keep up the

Young John McLoughlin, Dr. John's son. This son worried the entire family with his hot temper and recklessness. Nevertheless, Dr. John loved him and authorized Uncle Simon to spend large sums of money on the boy's education.
OREGON HISTORICAL SOCIETY

work of his fort. "I have a Duty," he said, "and with the Blessing of God will perform it to the utmost of my abilities and means." He sent Chief Trader Manson to take charge of the Stikine post, aided by three officers and six choice men. The tragedy would not be repeated, not if he could help it.

Day by day, week by week, he couldn't forget that young John was gone. "To Die is the fate of all," he wrote to a friend. "But to lose ones Son in the Way we lost him is more than painfull it is a Rack to ones feeling."

Goaded by grief and anger, he resolved to clear his son's name, so he checked the evidence again and again. The more he learned, the more certain he felt that Sir George had been unfair, and he finally wrote in fury,

"Instead of conducting the examination so as to endeavour to find out what had led to the murder, you conducted it as if it had been an investigation into the moral conduct of the Deceased, and as if you were desirous to justify the conduct of the murderers."

He told the Committee what "turbulent men" he had been forced to send to Stikine, and that Simpson, by transferring Roderick Finlayson, had caused young John's death. Others thought so too. John Work, one of the ablest company officers, said that if Finlayson had been left there, the tragedy would not have occurred.

Evidence favoring John began to mount. One visitor to the post wrote he had not seen John take "a single glass." Fort records were found in excellent order. Young John's personal liquor allowance had been scarcely touched.

One of the Stikine workmen, Pierre Kanaquasse. came to Fort Vancouver and reported that he had seen young McLoughlin "elevated," but never drunk; that the men were angry because, for the sake of safety, he wouldn't let them receive Indian women within the post nor leave it at night; that the men had been "scaling the Picquets" to sneak out, and stealing from the stores to get presents for their Indian sweethearts. When John had them punished for this, all but one had signed a pledge to get rid of him. Kanaquasse called it deliberate murder, not self-defense, for when John fell at the first shot and was "writhing in the agonies of Death," Heroux had placed his foot on the young man's neck and had beaten in his head with a rifle.

Other witnesses said the son was not a drunkard, had not been cruel, that post accounts were up-to-date, that the Stikine was a place of extreme danger. The inventory of the fort showed an unusually small discrepancy of less than ten pounds.

At first the Committee accepted Simpson's version, but as evidence mounted, they began to change their minds. The secretary wrote to Sir George, "I have come to the conclusion that McLoughlin was not a habitual drunkard, that the punishments he inflicted . . . were not of excessive severity, and that he was very vigilant and strict in keeping the men to their duty day and night."

Simpson showed foresight in his plans for the Columbia District, because conditions were changing. The American population was growing, animals were being trapped out, and silk hats had become fashionable instead of beaver, causing fur prices to slump. But he made a mistake in leaving young John alone on the

Stikine. He jumped to a false conclusion, failed to prosecute the guilty, tarnished John's good name, and offered not a scrap of compassion. Although Simpson was loyal and sometimes helpful to his workers, he was quick to turn on anyone who crossed him, and when angered, he was ruthless. His conduct now measured the man: a business genius—a callous human being.

As for Dr. John, thinking day and night about the tragedy, he showed the same wearisome trait as when he heckled Uncle Simon about his contract. He examined every witness, poured over letters and journals, wrote a "thundering letter" that attacked Simpson. He harped on the story until the Governor and Committee were sick of it, he harangued his own officers until they began to avoid him, and some of them, including James Douglas, started to correspond privately, behind McLoughlin's back, with Sir George Simpson. Perhaps it was necessary. Dr. John was so absorbed in trouble that his management of the fort was suffering.

Meanwhile, no matter what evidence turned up, Sir George clung angrily to his original belief. In any such contest the Committee would have to support the governor, because they needed him to supervise the company. In addition, the crime involved citizens of many nations—Iroquois, Kanakas (Hawaiians), Scots and Canadians. Canada felt unable to act because it didn't own Fort Stikine. The Russians said it was out of their hands because they had leased the land.

When Dr. John sent Heroux (who had fired the shot) and Kanaquasse (the Stikine workman) and eleven others to York Factory, the Governor and Com-

mittee censured him for sending so many so far without permission. They also decided that if the men were taken to England for trial, as Dr. John asked, he must personally bear the costs, more than ten thousand pounds, which was so expensive that he had to drop the case.

Humiliated, angry, grieving, Dr. John longed for consolation. He had many ties with the Catholics, for he had been baptized in that faith, his favorite sister was a nun, and the missionary priests of the coast were his friends. On a trip to Fort Nisqually he read a Catholic book called *The End of Controversy*, which seemed to promise just what he needed. Therefore, in the hands of young Father Blanchet, he accepted the Catholic faith and had his marriage to Marguerite sanctified. Solemn and dignified, thick white hair hanging to his collar, he knelt at the altar to receive his first communion at a Christmas midnight mass in the candle-lighted chapel at Fort Vancouver, while two choirs chanted alternately in French and Chinook jargon. For the rest of his life his religion was an inexpressible comfort.

But the bitter clash with Sir George was the turning point of his career. When 1841 opened, he had been

St. Paul's Mission in Willamette Valley, near Champoeg, was painted by Kane in the 1840s. This, the first Catholic mission in the northwest, was established by Dr. John's friend, Father Francis Blanchet, who later received him into the church.
ROYAL ONTARIO MUSEUM

at his peak. Now he was defeated, sorrowing, losing prestige, forced to back down on every front. He couldn't punish his son's murderers. He must change his beloved headquarters and give up his chain of forts. He was told to make up his quarrel with Sir George, or retire, or move to another department.

He would have to swallow that stiff Scotch-Irish pride.

FOURTEEN

Seeking Laws, Seeking Land

1842-1843

BACK in July, 1841, the year after Waller put up a mission on Dr. John's land, a carpenter named Felix Hathaway had built a cabin on the island part of the claim. He was not a missionary, although they sometimes hired him.

Dr. John was paddled across the channel to look it over. "Pilferer!" he shouted, with a thump of his cane. "Get—get out!"

It was his island. He had claimed it first, as everyone well knew. He ordered a small house to be erected on it and went home in a rage.

Hathaway abandoned the cabin. But in October, 1842, a few months after young John's murder, a group

Dr. John in late middle age. Very high stiff collars, called "stocks," worn with wide silk cravats, were the utmost in fashion. OREGON HISTORICAL SOCIETY

mainly from the mission formed the Island Milling Company and brought in a sawmill.

Again McLoughlin loudly ordered them off and reminded them of his claim. They refused to go. Hathaway had given them "title" in a pious deed in which he promised to defend the island against all persons, "the Lord excepted," and they chose to believe the "title" was good.

Dr. John then strengthened his own title as best he could by building a sawmill and hiring a surveyor to lay out a town which he named Oregon City. It was on three levels separated by high stone bluffs, with his land on the first two. He sold some lots, gave some away, and the village began to grow. Later it became the first incorporated town west of the Missouri River and capital of the whole West Coast.

But Waller hadn't quit. When he heard that Dr. John had donated a lot to a settler, he spluttered, "Tell him that I am much obliged to him for giving away lots on *my land*." He and the other missionaries refused to use the name Dr. John had chosen, and called the town only "The Falls."

That same autumn, 1842, a large group from the States, ragged and hollow-cheeked, plodded on horseback into the muddy street of Oregon City. Although Dr. John's company had told him to retard American settlement in any way he could, he pitied the newcomers, hired some and gave others goods on credit, doing more for them than their own countrymen were able to.

This first large immigration brought a big change, for they settled in Willamette Valley, shifting the focus of life from Fort Vancouver to Oregon City. They weakened Dr. John's influence and added to the number who wanted to form a government. In February 1843, the pro-government forces called two mass meetings where they discussed a problem that interested everyone—wolves! They also appointed a committee to draw up a plan for a government and present it to another meeting in May in Champoeg, the trading center of French Prairie.

At first Dr. John sympathized because he knew the Americans needed a way to keep peace among themselves. However, when he heard about a petition they had sent to the United States Congress, his sympathy turned to anger. "Never!" he thundered. "Never again will I do a favor for any man who signed!"

Directed against Dr. John and his company, this, the "Shortess petition," was a mixture of true and false, with much left out.

It said Dr. John lent cows—true. It also said he required the settlers to pay for cows that died—false. It accused him of challenging the Island Milling Company—true. But it didn't say he had claimed the island first, or mention joint occupancy, which gave him the same rights as any American. It said his measure of wheat was oversize—true. But it didn't explain that it was a standard Canadian measure, or that when the wheat weighed more, he paid more for it. Neither did it mention his countless helps to both missionaries and settlers. Many signers said later that they had been new in the country, had been "imposed upon," and thought the petition only a request for an American government.

Big Joe Meek, once a trapper, became a farmer in Willamette Valley. He was the one who called for the 1842 Champoeg meeting to divide and be counted, for or against forming a government. Later he became a United States marshal in the Oregon Territory. OREGON HISTORICAL SOCIETY

Dr. John didn't attend the Champoeg meeting on May 2, 1843, but more than a hundred settlers did, including some of his loyal Canadians.

It was a noisy, crowded session. One bearded settler made a motion to form a government. Men shouted their ayes and nays. The bespectacled secretary, George LeBreton, then suggested that they divide and be counted, and big Joe Meek, mountain-man-turned-farmer, led them into two lines. They counted—and the motion carried.

Almost all the French Canadians voted against it, because they would rather be governed by Dr. John. Afterward, as one writer expressed it, "the priest and his band (the Canadians) slunk away into the corners of the fences, and in a short time mounted their horses and left." Those who stayed elected a committee to draft some laws.

This was only one of many steps in forming a government, but it was important because it made the decision to unite. Even though Dr. John wasn't there, he knew what had happened, and realized he couldn't rule these rambunctious Yankees. But maybe his own French Canadians could hold them back. It was fortunate he had helped them settle in the Valley.

"The American population of the Wallamette had a political meeting last May and invited the Canadians to unite with them," he wrote. "The Canadians . . . told them they would positively take no part in their plans . . . so far, I am happy to say, everything is quiet."

As the next step, the settlers again gathered on the

prairie in July to hear the laws their committee had drafted. Many Americans had come, a few French Canadians, and Dr. John's oldest son Joe. Article by article they accepted the laws, with Joe making the motion to adopt one.

But Joe couldn't have approved the land law, for it said that every white male could have one square mile, which could not include any town site, nor extensive water power. It was frankly aimed at Dr. John, and if it passed, he would have to give up Oregon City and the falls. They would go instead to Waller and his group, because the law exempted "any claim of any mission . . . of an extent not greater than six miles square."

Dr. John had friends who hotly objected. He also had enemies who thought his British company ought to be driven out. Men grew angry—shouted—talked all at once. In the end, his friends were voted down.

When Dr. John heard about it he was dumfounded, for it would protect everyone's claim—except his.

If it became permanent, the Reverend Waller and the mission and the mission-backed Island Milling Company would receive all of his land.

FIFTEEN

The Horse Canoes

1843-1844

IN the fall of 1843 a ragged stranger burst into the fort. Hordes of travelers were upriver, he said, freezing and starving. Unless they received help, many would die.

Although Dr. John might have refused in revenge for the unjust new laws, he couldn't bear to let people suffer, so he sent voyageurs up the Columbia Gorge with a boatload of food. The stranger, James Waters, who was one of the immigrants, went along as guide and "sold" the food—a sale without money, on credit freely given to all. Many never paid.

Later, Indians brought word from tribe to tribe that one party was lost in the barren headwaters of the Snake River. White hair streaming, Dr. John rushed around "like one wild," called for his most capable men, and sent them out with provisions. After two weeks, when the rescuers finally found the lost camp, women ran to them and fell to their knees, weeping. Even the men cried and blessed the voyageurs and the kindly doctor who had sent them.

During that winter, which was unusually cold, with wind howling off snow-capped Mt. Hood and rain freezing to the gunwales, Dr. John repeatedly furnished boats and food. His men found one large party windbound on a raft and living on rawhide, and others up to their knees in slush. They fed them, wrapped them in blankets, and took them to the fort.

This, the "Great Emigration," was the first to drive wagons through. Small groups had come by sea, or overland by horseback, or down the river by Hudson's Bay boats. Those of the year before had left their wagons at Fort Hall and continued as a pack train.

But these nearly nine hundred souls had been determined to bring their possessions. They had chopped a road through the forested Blue Mountains, and when they reached the Dalles, on the Columbia, they had cut pines and made twenty-foot rafts. After taking off the wheels, they loaded their wagons on the rafts. Sometimes one wagon box became a shelter for the women and children, and one baby was born in such a "cabin."

It rained—snowed. Many ran out of food. The river was rough. They later said they endured more hardships coming down the Columbia than on all the rest of the trip together. Except for Dr. John's help, many would have perished.

When these bedraggled, dirty, famished people

Pioneers rafting down the Columbia on the last leg of their journey. In this picture the trip seems peaceful, but actually it was often rough, windy, cold and wet. The pioneers had to go ashore to camp at night, and one woman wrote about wading in slush up to her ankles, barefoot because her feet were so swollen she couldn't put on her shoes. OREGON HISTORICAL SOCIETY

reached the fort, they were astounded, for they had read false reports of Hudson's Bay cruelty and expected to find a monstrous establishment led by an ogre, ready to destroy them. Instead, here was a huge, kindly, white-haired gentleman, with a booming voice and slight stammer. He fed them, housed them until they could build huts or move in with friends; he gave them clothing, seed and implements on credit, and lent them cattle and hogs. If they were ill, he put them in his hospital.

One settler, William Beagle, had typhus fever. McLoughlin had Dr. Barclay fix up a house for the Beagle family, give them food, and take care of the sick man. Two months later, when Beagle was better, he asked Dr. John for his bill.

"Tut, tut, tut! Bill, bill, bill! Take care of yourself, sir! That is all the bill!" said Dr. John.

"It's too much. You can't afford to care for us so long without pay!" exclaimed Beagle.

"Tut, tut, tut! You do the best you can for some other man who is in trouble, and that will pay me!" McLoughlin sent the family to the valley in company canoes and sold them supplies on credit.

Many such incidents were recorded in settlers' journals. In doing this, Dr. John had two motives. The first was kindness. He couldn't let these people suffer, and he wanted them to raise a great deal of food, for if still more followed, even mighty Fort Vancouver couldn't keep them all alive.

His second motive was good business. These Yankees might be ragged and dirty, hollow-eyed, hungry, but they were also young and strong and had brought their families. While Fort Vancouver stood nearby, rich with food and clothing, these men would not see their children starve. Dr. John's fort must open its stores, or they would take it by storm.

Besides adding to the population, this influx alarmed the Indians. The Walla Walla chief Peu-peu-mox-mox came downriver in his long dugout canoe to talk over his worries.

Peu-peu-mox-mox, "Yellow Serpent," a great chief of the Walla Wallas, and Dr. John's friend. By calming the fears of Peu-peu-mox-mox, Dr. John helped keep the Indians from attacking immigrant wagon trains. ROYAL ONTARIO MUSEUM

"The Americans have no warlike aims," Dr. John told him, "and if they did, the British would not help them."

Peu-peu-mox-mox went back in peace, but others

came, and Dr. John repeatedly quieted their fears.

By now the Americans wanted the west coast and were convinced they had a right to it. Senator Mangum of North Carolina declared there was not "in the Senate or in the country a single anti-war man." Newspapers proclaimed, "The American Eagle is flapping his wings." "There must be no arbitration but at the cannon's mouth."

Because the Hudson's Bay Company stood in their way, almost all the articles and speeches were hostile toward it, and often toward Dr. John himself. They accused the company of mistreating settlers and slaughtering "hundreds of defenseless Indians." People chanted the slogan, "Fifty-four forty or Fight!" which meant a demand for all territory to the Alaskan border.

The British were equally determined to keep everything north of the Columbia. Parliament was openly talking about war, and one member stated, "England knows her rights and dares maintain them."

Dr. John was the man in the middle. With the United States, England and the Indians all spoiling for a fight, the place they would meet was right there on the Columbia.

Dr. John's dispute with Waller had stopped the growth of Oregon City, because neither man had a clear enough title to sell lots. Some Americans sympathized with Waller, others with McLoughlin. One of them, Dr. Elijah White, said, "If anyone not connected with the Hudson's Bay Company had been at half the pain and expense to establish a claim at the Willamette Falls, very few would have raised an opposition."

Dr. John couldn't bring suit, because there were no courts. Finally, as a last resort, he and Waller called in arbitrators, both American and British, including James Douglas. After some hard bargaining, Waller saw that his claim wouldn't stand up, and he decided to quit it, if Dr. John would pay him five acres and five hundred dollars, plus fourteen lots for the Methodist Mission. This was so high that the Americans themselves rejected it until Douglas won them over.

When Dr. John heard the terms, he gasped and looked toward the Americans. "Gentlemen, you have bound me!" he exclaimed.

They denied it, so he turned toward Douglas. "This is your doings!"

"Yes," Douglas replied. "I thought it best for your sake to give you one good fever and have done with it." He had concluded that the way to quiet Waller once and for all was to buy him off for a "handsome price."

Dr. John paid it, money and land. There, he thought. He had not only claimed it, he had bought it too. That should make it safe.

But his troubles weren't over, because the mission itself was crumbling and would soon close. The missionaries offered to sell Dr. John his own fourteen lots for six thousand dollars, reserving two for the church.

"This—this is an outrage!" spluttered Dr. John. He had just donated them! It was ridiculous to make him buy his own land! Most especially ridiculous to ask him to pay for Waller's house, built with his own timbers! But they would consent to nothing less, so McLoughlin finally agreed.

About this time, in the summer of 1844, the new immigrants cast their first votes, making many improvements in the government. For Dr. John, the most important was a change in the land law, which now would let him keep Oregon City.

He had publicly claimed that site, filed his claim, and had it surveyed. He had bought out both Waller and the mission. The new law favored him. At last surely he had clear possession. The milling company still held the island, but the town was his.

In the autumn rains immigrants again came down the Columbia, about fourteen hundred this year. As before, Dr. John had many of them brought downriver in company boats and saved them from freezing or starving. Thanks to his past loans of seed and implements, the colony had raised enough food for everyone, but the earlier immigrants had bought all the new clothes. Women patched and darned, and made shirts and jackets from canvas wagon covers. McLoughlin always had extra trading goods on hand, sealed for the following year. Now he thought the people's needs were more important than company rules, so he broke the seals.

Christmas came and passed.

Dr. John's terrible year was at hand.

SIXTEEN

The Terrible Year

1845

NOBODY knew what country would finally receive Oregon City. If the United States, only individuals could claim land, which meant Dr. John could hold it, but his company couldn't. Therefore, to safeguard the title and prove that he himself owned it, in March, 1845, he sent Sir George personal drafts for about twenty thousand dollars. With this, he had planted a time bomb.

That same spring two young Americans crossed the river and put up a hut on a Hudson's Bay pasture. Even though American officials helped run them off, Dr. John was worried, for immigrants were swarming in, and the next clash might be worse.

To be on the safe side, he renewed his fort stockade and built a blockhouse at one corner with eight

Fort Vancouver, about 1854, looking toward snow-capped Mt. Hood. Inside the stockade, the large house at its left corner is Dr. John's. The long building to right is Bachelors' Hall. The houses at the top of the knoll, in front of the trees, are United States officers' quarters, built after the Hudson's Bay Company left. Many of the other trees are orchards, planted while Dr. John was in charge. OREGON HISTORICAL SOCIETY

openings for cannon. When the settlers saw the pickets being repaired and the smiths making small arms for trade, they spread a report that the British were arming the Indians for war. It was preposterous, of course. If Dr. John had wanted to get rid of them he easily could have—by doing nothing and letting the Indians and the river finish them off. Instead he had saved all he could.

Dr. John was still loyal to Britain. "If you would not lose the country, you must protect your rights here," he had written, and asked, and asked again, for assistance.

Now he received his answer. "No such protection can be obtained. . . . You must therefore make use of the best means within your power for the preservation of the Company's rights."

It was all up to him.

One day when Dr. John went to the Falls, Jesse Applegate, member of the legislature, invited him to join the new government, called "Provisional" because the area wasn't yet legally American. Dr. John had been invited before, but refused to take the required oath of loyalty to the United States. Now the oath had been changed to a simple pledge to support the laws while remaining a dutiful "citizen of the United States or a subject of Great Britain." He could promise this with honor, so he took the new oath, expecting to pay taxes and receive support.

Ironically, now that he no longer needed help, a British warship arrived in Puget Sound with orders to protect Her Majesty's subjects. Two of her men, Captain Parke and Lieutenant Peel, came to Fort Vancouver.

Parke was a belligerent young fellow, eager to take on the Americans. He talked about bringing troops overland from Canada and said that if it came to blows, "We will hit them a good deal harder than we would other people."

The only known picture of William Glen Rae, Eloisa's husband, on a gold bracelet that belonged to her. It is now at the McLoughlin House (a museum) in Oregon City.

Dr. John, shaking his white head, replied, "O Captain Parke! Captain Parke!"

He sent the young men across the river to see for themselves how strong the Yankees were, and how determined to hang onto the area. Convinced, Lieutenant Peel went posthaste back to England with a report on American strength, a letter from Dr. John to the ship's Captain Gordon, and one from the captain saying the country was "not worth five straws." Peel's report, which had been influenced by Dr. John, was important. The British Foreign Office took it seriously.

Dr. John was worried about his family, too. He had been ordered years before to close Yerba Buena on San Francisco Bay, where his son-in-law had set up a post. William Glen Rae was handsome, romantic, in-

Eloisa and her daughter, Mary Angelique Harvey. Eloisa had six children. John, Margaret and Maria Louisa Rae; Daniel, James, and Mary Angelique Harvey. All of them lived in Dr. John's home in Oregon City, and the Harvey children were born there. MCLOUGHLIN MEMORIAL ASSOCIATION

telligent, but never a strong character. Rumor whispered that he had threatened Eloisa's life and the lives of the children, and drank too much. Although Yerba Buena wasn't doing well, McLoughlin had hoped against hope that Rae would succeed, but at last he sent word that it must be closed.

In June, however, before his orders could have reached California, shocking news arrived. Rae had taken his own life.

Dr. John was crushed. His son John—murdered. Rae —a suicide. Eloisa—a widow with three small children. Must everyone he loved be destroyed by this wild life of the fur trade? Grieving, he sent his youngest son David to help close Yerba Buena and had Eloisa and her children come to the fort.

He still brooded about the Stikine, and he was filling his reports with blasts at Simpson. Even though the Governor and Committee knew Simpson had behaved badly, they were tired of hearing about it. They were also displeased because expenses at the Falls were heavy, because Dr. John had not closed Yerba Buena when he was told to, and because the Puget Sound Agricultural Company was not paying. Therefore they decided to split his Columbia District and end his special bonus of five hundred pounds a year.

At this time Sir George Simpson wrote a memorandum to the British government about the Oregon situation, after which the government had him send out two observers. They were Lieutenants Henry Warre and Mervin Vavasour, supposed to look for west coast military sites in case of war, and to find out how the

American settlers and Hudson's Bay personnel felt about such a war. Posing as tourists, these men bought "superfine beaver hats, figured vests, tweed trousers, fine handkerchiefs, pipes, and extract of roses" from the fort store. They saw American farms strung out along the rivers, and Yankees busy laying out roads, plotting town sites, and starting schools.

Back in London their report blamed Dr. John for aiding the missionaries, immigrants, and Provisional Government. Without McLoughlin, it said, "not thirty American families would now have been in the settlement. The first Immigration . . . arrived in so miserable a condition that had it not been for the trading posts of the Hudson's Bay Company they must have been starved or been cut off by the Indians."

This report was known to the Hudson's Bay Governor and Committee in London, honorable men who had at first told Dr. John to assist anyone who needed it. But now they were alarmed at the growing American population, and they lived too far away to see that he couldn't possibly keep the immigrants out. So they believed the Warre and Vavasour report and were especially horrified because Dr. John had advanced the settlers thirty-two thousand dollars, which Simpson called "an enormous sum."

As this, the last straw, company officers accepted Dr. John's offer to pay for the Falls—the time bomb. They told him he was no longer superintendent of the Columbia, but was replaced by a three-man board consisting temporarily of himself, James Douglas, and Peter Skene Ogden. They also said that after so many years as ruler of Fort Vancouver, it might cause "embarrassment" if he stayed there merely as a member of the board. To prevent this, next year he would be sent to a different post "across the mountains."

As expected, this put Dr. John in an impossible position. Only residents could hold a claim, so if he accepted a transfer, he would lose his land. He must either abandon Oregon City, for which he had just paid twenty thousand dollars—or resign. Obviously they wanted him to quit. Otherwise they would have given him a chance to withdraw his offer and get his money back.

He could hardly believe it. The American Fur Company, the North West Company, earlier Hudson's Bay chief factors—all had tried and failed to build a strong post on the Columbia. Only he had succeeded. He had developed fields—herds—mills. He had founded forts, managed ships, made friends with the natives, figured out what to buy and sell and produce. He had kept peace with the Americans. All the day-by-day decisions had been his.

And now he was being maneuvered out of his job. He brooded, felt "disgraced and degraded," said he hadn't meant the offer to buy the Falls, wrote long stormy letters dwelling on his grievances. Everywhere he looked he faced trouble. His son and son-in-law were killed. Americans, whom he had befriended, had turned against him. His men, writing to Sir George, seemed disloyal. He had quarreled with the governor of his company, lost his position. It had all started with Sir George's visit. That, he said, "has cost me Dear."

When he was shown the Warre-Vavasour report, he wrote a long, sorrowful, yet noble, defense.

Accused of being a friend to the missionaries, he replied, "What would you have? Would you have me turn the cold shoulder to the men of God who came to do that for the Indians which the company had neglected to do?"

He said he had to join the Provisional Government for protection "while the dogs of war were snarling and threatening."

He said he had aided the immigrants to keep them from perishing of starvation. "If we had not done this, Vancouver would have been destroyed, and the world would have judged us treated as our inhuman conduct deserved . . . and the trouble which would have arisen in consequence would have probably involved the British and American nations in war."

As for getting rid of the settlers, he reminded the Committee that "we have no Right or Power to drive them away."

The terrible year, 1845, was almost over. In March Dr. John had sent Simpson drafts to pay for the Falls. In June he heard of Rae's suicide, and learned that his district was to be split, his pay cut. In the fall he was told that his drafts were accepted, and he was to be transferred. Grieving, humiliated, driven away from the fort he loved, he asked for a furlough.

"I have Drunk and am Drinking the cup of Bitterness to the very Dregs," he wrote, his great shoulders bowed.

Dr. John was a passionate, stubborn, often difficult

man who had undoubtedly brought some of his troubles on himself, yet he was also a great and good man, gifted with foresight and overwhelming kindness. Many who knew him called him "noble," and countless letters, diaries and newspaper articles told of his generosity and his people's affection. He had compassion for everyone, Catholic and Protestant and pagan, red-skinned and white.

Caught in a clash between two nations, in a world that was changing fast, he had steered the area through its time of danger, keeping the peace in a hundred small ways and working with the American leaders to lay a foundation that would last until the boundary was settled. If a mean-spirited man had been at the helm, if he had been severe with the settlers, or quarreled with their leaders, Americans might have attacked the fort. If he had not reassured the Indians, they would surely have risen, which would have brought in American troops. Both countries were ready to fight, and any violence might have ignited the fuse.

To the end of his life Dr. John was convinced he had prevented a British-American war.

SEVENTEEN

A Dieu

1846-1857

WHILE Dr. John was waiting for the weary year to end, he had a house built in Oregon City, the finest house there, near the Falls and his mills. Painted white, it was two stories tall, with a dignified central entrance and high windows. There he had his beautiful furniture moved—mahogany table, silver candlesticks, blue and white dishes. No more would they gleam in the firelight at Fort Vancouver while his guests drank from crystal glasses, and course after course was passed around. All that was over and done.

The last settlers were brought safely down the Gorge, Christmas was over, and the New Year beginning. On January 6, 1846, Dr. John climbed into a bateau.

Row brothers row, the stream runs fast,
The rapids are near and the daylight's past.

For the last time voyageurs sang for Dr. John as chief of Fort Vancouver, and eleven days later, when he had the house ready, Marguerite, Eloisa and the children set out to join him. If he returned to the company, it would be to another post.

All day in Oregon City he could hear the roar of the falls, whine of mills, screech of slow-moving ox-carts past his door. Canoes and flatboats were beached nearby. Already the settlement had five hundred people with eighty houses, two churches, two taverns, many shops, mills and the brand-new *Spectator*, first American newspaper on the Pacific Coast. Dr. John could be proud of this thriving town.

In addition, his company had been generous. It hadn't charged him any costs from young John's murder or debts of settlers. His special salary of five hundred pounds was continued for one extra year; this year was a furlough followed by two years' leave of absence at full pay, making his formal retirement begin June 1, 1849. After that he was to receive, as all retiring chief factors did, full pay for one more year and half pay for five.

Nevertheless, after so many years as ruler of Fort Vancouver Dr. John found it a terrible change to be a private citizen and frequently disliked, for many Americans resented him as British, well-to-do and Catholic. He was so lonely and bitter that his friends were worried about his "desponding state," and were afraid he might "lose his reason."

But Dr. John gradually became interested in his new life. Although he rented his sawmills, he ran his own flour mill. He had business contacts in Montreal and the Sandwich Islands, ordered goods direct from the Hudson's Bay Company in London and tried to open markets for lumber and wheat as far away as Tahiti and Manila. Before long he notified the company that he would not return when his furlough was over.

Dr. John was happier now. His big house rang with children's laughter, for Eloisa lived there too, at first with her three little ones, and later, after she remarried, with several more. McLoughlin loved children and indulged them. One small neighbor, who sat beside him on a horsehair sofa at a wedding, never forgot her delight because Dr. John, seeing how wistful she looked, gave her a tiny sip of his wine.

By now so many settlers had come to the Northwest that both countries felt the boundary must be decided. At one time the Americans had been ready to fight for the far north, but in 1845 the republic of

Dr. John with the daughters of Eloisa and William Glen Rae. Margaret, left, was born on the ship Beaver *while her parents were returning to Fort Vancouver from the Stikine. Louisa, right, was Dr. John's favorite. From the ages of twelve to fifteen she wrote letters to his dictation because he had arthritis and couldn't handle a pen. She made two copies of each, and if she made a blot or mistake he had her recopy the entire page.* OREGON HISTORICAL SOCIETY

Texas entered the Union, starting the Mexican War, and the United States didn't want trouble on two fronts.

The English had also once been ready to fight. Now, because the potato and wheat crops in Britain had failed, they needed cheap food from America. Besides that, some of their messengers, such as young Lieutenant Peel, had told the Home Office how strong and determined the Yankees were.

No very great area was in question. The British had long ago given up much hope of holding anything south of the Columbia. Even though Americans talked about "Fifty-four forty or Fight!" the United States had been offering the forty-ninth parallel ever since the days of Thomas Jefferson. This left a triangle from that parallel to the Columbia, from the Rockies to the Pacific. Mexican War or none, the Americans would fight for that much, and the British decided it wasn't worth a conflict. So in 1846 the line was drawn, making the triangle part of America.

The new addition, called the Oregon Territory, included the present states of Oregon, Washington and Idaho, and part of Montana and Wyoming. The United States now extended from the Atlantic to the Pacific.

Overjoyed to have the long quarrel ended at last, Dr. John prepared to become a loyal citizen of his adopted country. He hoped the government would "soon be here to maintain order and Establish the Rights of Individuals," and was confident that his property would be safe. After all, the treaty explicitly said the rights "of the Hudson's Bay Company and of all British Subjects . . . shall be respected."

Two years earlier, even before Oregon became a territory, Dr. John had asked his American friend Peter Burnett, Justice of the Peace, to give him the oath of citizenship.

"I haven't the authority," Burnett had replied, for he held office under the Provisional Government. Dr. John had to wait until the Mexican War was over, giving the United States another huge chunk of land. Then Congress had time to think about Oregon, and in 1849 Governor Joseph Lane came to organize the territory, with W. P. Bryant as the first territorial judge.

Dr. John didn't dally. Picking up his cane, he went to Judge Bryant, took the oath of allegiance and declared that he intended to become an American citizen. He was pleased with his new status, sure his adopted country would treat him fairly, and didn't realize the judge was part of a conspiracy against him.

Judge Bryant had bought the logs and mill on Dr. John's island from George Abernethy, who had been governor under the Provisional Government, and was a member of the so-called "Mission Party." This party wasn't connected with any mission or church, although some of its leaders had been missionaries.

The Mission Party backed Samuel R. Thurston, an ambitious newcomer, as delegate to the United States Congress. Dr. John had openly voted against the Mission candidate, but Thurston was elected and set out for Washington, D.C. He was too new to understand the complicated land claim, but he knew quite well what his backers wanted—Dr. John's island.

Oregon had one overriding need—a land law—and

Oregon City, in 1845, a sketch made by Lieutenant Warre of the Warre-Vavasour investigation. The falls, Dr. John's house, and his mill, are just out of the picture to the right.

Today the town stands on both levels, and the bluffs are so high that a civic elevator carries pedestrians from one section to the other. OREGON HISTORICAL SOCIETY

Judge Bryant went to Washington, too, to help Thurston get such a law passed. This meant that both Oregon men at the Capitol, the federal judge and federal delegate, were Dr. John's enemies. Judge Bryant had bought the island and was determined to keep it. The delegate, Thurston, owed his election to the Mission Party, and also resented Dr. John for voting against him.

Hints soon drifted back to Oregon City that they were planning to seize all of McLoughlin's land. This was because the island had been part of the original claim, and if Dr. John received title to any, it might establish a precedent which would give him the island too.

A letter which Thurston sent to Congress was published in the Oregon City *Spectator*. It called McLoughlin the "chief fugleman" for the Hudson's Bay Company, said he had driven the mission from "their" claim, had "refused" to become a citizen and had realized more than two hundred thousand dollars from the property, "enough for a foreigner to make out of American territory."

Horrified, Dr. John replied that he could "scarcely believe anyone would write such a mass of lies," that he had made only twenty thousand dollars from sale of lots, and that he had donated more than three hundred lots to various churches. But Thurston and Bryant were able to convince Congress that Dr. John was a greedy, conniving Britisher and persuaded it to pass a land law which confirmed all titles except the "Oregon City Claim" (McLoughlin's). This was given to the territory, to be sold, and the proceeds used for a university, but the island was exempted and awarded to Judge Bryant.

Every settler in Oregon received title to his land—except Dr. John. Crushed, he found that all he owned was to be taken away. He was to be paid nothing, not even for his mills and shops, not even for his home.

At first the settlers were wildly jubilant to have their own claims confirmed. However, a reaction soon set in, for people knew that Dr. John had not only claimed the land first, but had bought it too, and that the boundary settlement should protect his rights. Thurston's own party began to mention other possible delegates. The Methodist Church strongly criticized him. Newspapers printed letters of protest.

In every respect, except his treatment of Dr. John, Thurston was an upright man, but he was hungry for office and had not lived in the west long enough to understand the land claim. Most of his friends thought that if he had not died at sea on his way back to Oregon, he would have had the law changed to give McLoughlin fair play.

Judge Bryant, who had been in Oregon even a shorter time than Thurston, soon transferred the island back to Abernethy. Some historians have called their conduct "questionable." Others have bluntly said that giving Bryant title to the island amounted to a bribe.

The Hudson's Bay Company had already begun to transfer headquarters to Fort Victoria, farther north, and by now James Douglas and most of Dr. John's other friends had moved away, leaving only a few men at the old fort. Soon it became a post of the United States

Army, which put up its own buildings and let the old ones decay.

Population in the territory continued to grow. Every year settlers poured into the upper valley. Every year more oxcarts rumbled along the portage road around the falls, carrying goods upriver and wheat to market. Dozens of steamboats laced together the towns and farms, for roads were scarce.

Dr. John tried to be a good citizen and was elected mayor, but served for only a few months, then resigned. He could take no pleasure in his prosperous little city. Stubborn to the end, he wrote a petition for return of his land, secured signers and sent it to Washington, to no effect. Congress had larger concerns than injustice to one old man in the far west, and besides, the territorial delegate and territorial judge had helped draft the very law of which he complained.

Dr. John was heartbroken. Dressed in a long blue swallowtail coat with brass buttons, a high beaver hat, beaded Indian moccasins, and carrying his gold-headed cane, he paced the dusty street. He stopped anyone he met to indulge in violent tirades against the mission, the government, the settlers who had forgotten him. He

Interior of Fort Vancouver, a photograph taken about 1860, after the Hudson's Bay Company had left. Dr. John's house, large and comfortable, still retains its picket fence and steps to the veranda. The tripod holds the fort bell which rang out the hours, and the long building is the famous Bachelors' Hall.
OREGON HISTORICAL SOCIETY

brandished his cane, shouted. Sometimes, ashamed of his outburst, he broke off abruptly and murmured, "God forgive me."

Because the authorities knew how unjust the law was, they didn't turn him out of his property, so he continued to live in his house and manage his business. An employee, Daniel Harvey, married Eloisa and became McLoughlin's trusted assistant, while David, who had gone to the California gold fields, returned. Although the family ran the store, mills and shipping, they knew they could be dispossessed at any time.

In spite of his trouble, Dr. John didn't forget the needy. He sold goods freely on credit. His doors were never locked. He and Marguerite almost never left the house together, in case someone came for help, and more nights than not the two couches in the hall were occupied by men who had no other place to sleep.

But his joy in life had vanished. He lost so much weight that his great frame was gaunt and grim, his eyes sunken. He spent hours poring over old bills, arranging them in piles, figuring which he might be able to collect. By summer, 1857, he was bedfast.

One day Lafayette Grover, a promising young politician, rode on horseback through Oregon City, and when he passed Dr. John's house a messenger came from the doctor, asking him to call. He found McLoughlin in bed.

"I shall live but a little while longer; and this is the reason I sent for you," Dr. John told him. "I am an old man and just dying, and you are a young man and will live many years in this country. As for me, I might better have been shot!" He said the words harshly. "I might better have been shot forty years ago . . ."

As he paused, Grover too was silent. In a moment Dr. John continued, ". . . than to have lived here and tried to build up a family and an estate in this government. I became a citizen of the United States in good faith. I planted all I had here, and the government has confiscated my property. Now what I want to ask of you is that you will give your influence after I am dead to have this property go to my children. I have earned it as other settlers have earned theirs, and it ought to be mine and my heirs."

"I will favor your request," Grover promised.

On September 2, Dr. Henry DeChesne, Dr. John's nephew who was attending him, entered his bedroom where the family were gathered.

"*Comment allez-vous?*" asked Dr. DeChesne, for he and Dr. John used French with one another. This means "How are you?" but its literal translation is, "How are you going?"

Almost in a whisper Dr. John replied, "A *Dieu.*" (To God.)

They were his last words.

But the end was not quite yet, for many could not forget the injustice. Some of them, especially Lafayette Grover, worked to remedy it. Two years after McLoughlin's death, Oregon became a state. Three years after that, on October 17, 1862, the Oregon Legislature passed an act with only two nays in the Senate and none in the House. This act enabled Dr. John's heirs—Eloisa and her husband Daniel Harvey, for by then David had sold them his share and Marguerite had died—to purchase for one thousand dollars the land claim except Abernethy Island. This small payment was necessary because the federal law had said the claim must be sold and the proceeds given to the university.

Eloisa and Daniel could have paid it in paper money at a great discount, but they scorned to do this. Instead, when they came to claim their inheritance, they turned over the money in coins of gold.

Dr. John would have liked that.

It was worthy of the white-headed eagle.

Bibliography

This is not a complete bibliography of works on Dr. John and the early west. It includes only those I have used and found helpful.

BIBLIOGRAPHY

Primary Sources (Original journals, letters, reports, etc.)

Allen, Miss A. J. *Ten Years in Oregon: Travels and Adventures of Dr. E. White and Lady*. Ithaca, N.Y., 1850.

Bailey, Margaret Jewett Smith. *The Grains, or Passages in the Life of Ruth Roper, with Occasional Pictures of Oregon, Natural and Moral*. Portland, 1854.

Barker, Burt Brown, editor. *The Financial Papers of Dr. John McLoughlin*. Portland, 1949.

Barker, Burt Brown, editor. *The McLoughlin Empire and Its Rulers*. Glendale, California, 1959.

Blanchet, Francois. *Historical Sketches of the Catholic Church in Oregon*. Portland, 1878.

Beaver, Herbert. *Reports and Letters of Herbert Beaver, 1836–38*. Edited by Thomas E. Jessett. Portland, 1959.

Bonneville, Benjamin. *Captain Bonneville's Lost Report.* Annals of Wyoming, April, 1932, Vol. 8, #4. Cheyenne, 1932.

Burnett, Peter. *Recollections and Opinions of an Old Pioneer.* New York, 1880.

Cox, Ross. *Adventures on the Columbia River.* London, 1831. New York, 1832.

Crawford, Medorem. *Journal.* (37th Congress, 3rd Session, Sen. Ex. Document 17).

Douglas, David. *Journal Kept by David Douglas During His Travels in N. America.* N.Y. Antiquarian Press, 1959. Also in OHQ, V, 1904 and VI, 1905.

Dryden, Cecil. *Up the Columbia for Furs.* (Alexander Ross and Ross Cox Journals.) Caldwell, Idaho, 1949.

Dunn, John. *History of Oregon and British North American Fur Trade.* Philadelphia, 1845.

Edwards, Phillip Ligget. *Sketch of the Oregon Country, Emigrants' Guide.* Liberty, Missouri, 1842.

Edwards, Phillip Ligget. *California in 1837.* Sacramento, 1890.

Farnham, Thomas J., *Travels in the Great Western Prairies, the Anahuac and Rocky Mountains, and in the Oregon Territory.* New York, 1843.

Glazebrook, G. P. de T., editor. *The Hargrave Correspondence, 1821–1843.* Toronto, 1938.

Gray, W. H. *History of Oregon.* Portland, 1870.

Greenhow, Robert. *History of Oregon and California.* Boston, 1844, 1845.

Harmon, Daniel Williams. *A Journal of Voyages and Travels in the Interior of North America.* Toronto, 1911.

Hines, Reverend Gustavus. *Life on the Plains of the Pacific—Oregon: Its History, Condition and Prospects.* Buffalo, 1851.

Hines, H. K. *Missionary History of the Pacific North West,*

Containing the Wonderful Story of Jason Lee with Sketches of Many of His Labors. Published privately, 1899.

Hopkins, Flora. *Autobiography of John Ball.* Grand Rapids, 1925.

Kelley, Hall. *Hall J. Kelley on Oregon.* Princeton University, 1932. (Reprints of earlier published works.)

Lee, Daniel, and Frost, J. H. *Ten Years in Oregon.* New York, 1844.

Landerholm, Carl, editor and translator. *Notices and Voyages of the Famed Quebec Mission to the Pacific Northwest.* Portland, 1856.

McLoughlin, John. *The Financial Papers of Dr. John McLoughlin.* Edited by Burt Brown Barker. Portland, 1949.

McLoughlin, John. *McLoughlin's Fort Vancouver Letters.* Edited by E. E. Rich. Publications of the Champlain Society, Hudson's Bay Company Series. Toronto, the Champlain Society.

First Series, 1825–38. Vol. 4, 1941.
Second Series, 1839–44. Vol. 6, 1943.
Third Series, 1844–46. Vol. 7, 1944.

McLoughlin, John. *Letters of Dr. John McLoughlin Written at Fort Vancouver, 1829–1832.* Edited by Dr. Burt Brown Barker. Portland, 1948.

McLoughlin, John. *John McLoughlin's Business Correspondence, 1847–1848.* Edited by William R. Sampson, University of Washington, 1973.

Martin, Chester. *Lord Selkirk's Work in Canada.* Toronto, 1916.

Merk, Frederick. *Fur Trade and Empire.* Edited by Frederick Merk. (Journal of George Simpson, 1824–1825.) Cambridge, 1931.

Murray, John. *Statement Respecting the Earl of Selkirk's Settlement Upon the Red River.* London, 1817.

Ogden, Peter Skene. *Snake Country Journals.* Hudson's Bay Record Society, 3 vols. Edited by E. E. Rich, 1950; ed. by K. G. Davies, 1961; ed. by Slyndwr Williams, 1971. London.

O'Hara, E. V. *Pioneer Catholic History of Oregon.* St. Anthony Guild. Paterson, N.J., 1911.

Payette, B. C. *The Northwest.* Montreal, 1964.

Payette, B. C. *The Oregon Country under the Union Jack.* Montreal, 1962.

Robertson, Colin. *Colin Robertson's Correspondence Book, September 1817 to September 1822.* Ed. by E. E. Rich. Champlain Society, Hudson's Bay Series vol. II. Toronto, 1939.

Robinson, Henry Martin. *The Great Fur Land.* New York, 1879.

Ross, Alexander. *Adventures of the First Settlers on the Oregon or Columbia River.* London, 1849.

Simpson, Sir George. *Narrative of a Voyage to California Ports in 1841–1842.* Philadelphia, 1847.

Thornton, J. Quinn. *Oregon and California in 1848.* New York, 1849.

Tolmie, Dr. William Fraser. *The Journal of William Fraser Tolmie, Physician and Fur Trader.* Vancouver, 1963.

Townsend, John Kirk. *Narrative of a Journey Across the Rocky Mountains, to the Columbia River.* Cleveland, 1905.

Wallace, W. Stewart, ed. *Documents Relating to the Northwest Company.* The Champlain Society, Toronto, 1934.

White, Elijah. *A Concise View of Oregon Territory, Its Colonial and Indian Relations.* Washington, D.C., 1846.

Whitman, Narcissa. *Letters and Journal.* Compiled by T. C. Elliott. Portland, 1937.

Wilcocke, Samuel H. A *Narrative of Occurrences in the Indian Country.* London, 1817.

Wilkes, Charles. *Narrative of the United States Exploring Ex-*

pedition During the Years 1838, 1839, 1840, 1841, 1842. 5 vols. Philadelphia, 1849.

Wyeth, Nathaniel J. *The Correspondence and Journals of Captain Nathaniel J. Wyeth, 1831–6.* Eugene, Oregon, 1899.

MANUSCRIPTS

Note: OHS = Oregon Historical Society, Portland, Oregon.

DeChesne, Dr. Henry. Letters. In Eva Emery Dye papers. At OHS.

Ermatinger Papers, including letters from Dr. John McLoughlin. In special collections at University of British Columbia, Vancouver, B.C.

Harvey, Eloisa McLoughlin. Biography of John McLoughlin. Transcript at OHS, from original in Bancroft Library, Berkeley, California.

McGill University, class roll, medical class of 1834. Archives, McGill University, Montreal, Quebec.

McGillivray, Simon. Notebook Kept at Fort William, 1815. Copy at Old Fort William from original in Public Archives of Canada.

McLoughlin, David. Correspondence and papers. At OHS.

McLoughlin, Dr. John. Contract with McTavish, Frobisher & Co. Original notarial copy at Old Fort William. Original signed document at National Archives of Quebec at Montreal.

McLoughlin, John, Jr. Letters. In special collections at University of British Columbia, Vancouver, B.C.

McLoughlin family papers, misc. At OHS.

Selkirk, papers. "Inventory of Fort William." Copy at Old Fort William from original in Public Archives of Canada.

Selkirk, Lord. Plan of Fort William. Copy at Old Fort William from original in Ontario Archives.

Thornton, J. Quinn. Letters to Frances Fuller Victor. At OHS.
Victor, Frances Fuller. Papers. At OHS.

SECONDARY SOURCES (* = contains much primary material).

American Heritage Publication, *The Great West*. New York, 1965.

*Bancroft, H. H. *History of the Northwest*, 2 vols. San Francisco, 1884.

*Bancroft, H. H. History of Oregon, 2 vols. San Francisco, 1886, 1888.

*Brosnan, Cornelius J. *Jason Lee, Prophet of New Oregon*. N.Y., 1932.

Bryce, George. *History of Manitoba*. Toronto, Montreal, 1906.

Bryce, George. *The Remarkable History of the Hudson's Bay Company*. London, 1900.

Bryce, George. *The Romantic Settlement of Lord Selkirk's Colonists* (*The Pioneers of Manitoba*). Not dated.

Campbell, Marjorie Wilkins. *The North West Company*. New York. 1957.

Carey, Charles H. A *General History of Oregon Prior to 1861*. 2 vols. Portland, 1936.

Clark, Robert Carlton. *History of the Willamette Valley, Oregon*. 3 vols. Chicago, 1927.

Clark, D. E. *The West in American History*. Crowell, 1937.

*Clarke, Samuel A. *Pioneer Days of Oregon History*. 2 vols. N.Y., 1905.

Cogswell, Philip, Jr. *Capitol Names*. Portland, 1977.

Corning, Howard M. *Willamette Landings*. Portland, 1947.

Dillon, Richard. *The Siskiyou Trail*. N.Y., 1975.

Dobbs, Caroline C. *Men of Champoeg*. Portland, 1932.

Dye, Eva Emery. *McLoughlin and Old Oregon*. Chicago, 1900.

Eide, Ingvard Henry. *The Oregon Trail.* Chicago, New York, San Francisco, 1972.

*Gay, Theressa. *Life and Letters of Mrs. Jason Lee.* Portland, 1936.

Hill, Douglas. *The Opening of the Canadian West.* New York, 1967.

*Holman, Frederick V. *Dr. John McLoughlin.* Cleveland, 1907.

Hussey, J. A. *Champoeg: Place of Transition.* Portland, 1967.

Hussey, J. A. *The History of Fort Vancouver.* Portland, 1957.

Jenkins, Kathleen. *Montreal, Island City of the St. Laurence.* New York, 1966.

Johnson, Robert. *John McLoughlin, Patriarch of the North West.* Portland, 1935.

Landerholm, Carl. *Vancouver Area Chronology.* Vancouver, 1960.

*Laut, Agnes C. *The Conquest of the Great Northwest.* Toronto, not dated.

*Laut, Agnes C. *Conquest of our Western Empire.* New York, 1927.

Lavender, David. *Land of Giants.* New York, 1956.

Loewenberg, Robert J. *Equality on the Oregon Frontier.* University of Washington Press, 1976.

McKay, Douglas. *The Honorable Company.* New York, 1936.

Merk, Frederick. *The Oregon Question.* Harvard, 1967.

Montgomery, Richard. *The White-Headed Eagle.* New York, 1934.

Nute, Grace Lee. *The Voyageur.* St. Paul, 1931.

Rich, E. E. *The Fur Trade and the Northwest to 1857.* Toronto, 1967.

Schlesser, Norman Dennis. *Fort Umpqua–Bastion of Empire.* Roseburg, 1972.

*Scott, Harvey W. *History of the Oregon Country.* 6 vols. Cambridge, 1924.

*Skinner, Constance Lindsay. *Adventurers in Oregon*. Yale U. Press, 1920.

*Sullivan, M. S. *The Travels of Jedediah Smith*. Santa Ana, Calif., 1934.

Thompson, Erwin N. *Shallow Grave at Waiilatpu*. Portland, 1969.

*Victor, Frances Fuller. *The River of the West*. Hartford, Conn. and Toledo, Ohio, 1870.

Wrong, George M. *A Canadian Manor and Its Seigneurs*.

PERIODICALS

Note: OHQ = Quarterly of the Oregon Historical Society.
WHQ = Quarterly of the Washington Historical Society.
TOPA = Transactions of the Oregon Pioneer Association.
* = Primary source.

Allan, George T. "Reminiscences of Fort Vancouver." TOPA, 1881, 75–80.

Ball, John. "Across the Continent Seventy Years Ago." OHQ, III (March, 1902), 83–106.

*Beaver, Rev. Herbert. "Mr. Beaver Objects." *The Beaver*, September, 1941, 10–13.

The Beaver. Special issue, Autumn, 1970.

Bird, Annie Laurie. "Thomas McKay," and "The Will of Thomas McKay." OHQ, XL (March, 1939), 1–18.

Carey, Charles H. "Lee, Waller and McLoughlin." OHQ, XXXIII (September, 1932), 187–213.

Clark, Robert C. "How British and American Subjects Unite in Common Government for Oregon." OHQ, XIII (June, 1912), 140–159.

*Correspondence of John McLoughlin, Nathaniel J. Wyeth, S. R. Thurston, and R. C. Winthrop, Pertaining to Claim of Doctor McLoughlin." OHQ, I (March, 1900), 105–109.

Crawford, Medorem. "Address to the Oregon Pioneer Association." TOPA, 1881, 9–19.

*Duniway, David, and Riggs, Neil, editors. "The Oregon Archives, 1841–1843." OHQ, LX (June, 1959), 211–280.

Elliott, T. C. "Dr. John McLoughlin and His Guests." WHQ, III (October, 1908), 63–77.

Elliott, T. C. "Marguerite Wadin McKay McLoughlin." OHQ, XXXVI (December, 1935), 338–347.

*Elliott, T. C. "Peter Skene Ogden, Fur Trader." (Contains Ogden's Report.) OHQ, XI (September, 1910), 229–278.

*Ermatinger, Frank. "Diary." Edited by Eva Emery Dye. WHQ, I (January, 1907), 16–29.

Himes, George H. "Dr. John McLoughlin." TOPA, 1886, 41–58.

Holman, Fred V. "A Brief History of the Oregon Provisional Government." OHQ, XIII (June, 1912), 89–139.

*Knuth, Priscilla, editor. "H.M.S. *Modeste* on the Pacific Coast, 1843–47: Log and Letters." OHQ, LXI (December, 1960), 408–436.

*Lee, Jason. "Diary." OHQ, XVII (June, September, December, 1916), 116–146; 240–266; 397–430.

Lyman, Horace. "Dr. John McLoughlin." TOPA, 1886, 41–58.

*McLoughlin, Dr. John. "Answer to Report of Warre and Vavasour." OHQ, XXXIII (March, 1932), 214–229.

*McLoughlin, Dr. John. "Copy of a Document Found Among the Private Papers of the Late Dr. John McLoughlin." TOPA, 1880, 46–55.

*McLoughlin, Dr. John. "Documentary: Letter, Doctor John

McLoughlin to Sir George Simpson, March 20, 1844." Edited by Katharine Judson. OHQ, XVII (September, 1916), 215–239.

*McLoughlin, Dr. John. "Dr. John McLoughlin's Last Letter to the Hudson's Bay Company, 1845." Edited by Katharine Judson. *American Historical Review,* 21 (October, 1915), 104–134.

*McLoughlin, Dr. John. "Narrative of Events in Early Oregon Ascribed to Dr. John McLoughlin." OHQ, I (June, 1900), 193–206.

Matthieu, F. Xavier, "Reminiscences." OHQ, I (March, 1900), 73–104.

Minto, John. "What I Know of Dr. McLoughlin and How I Know It." OHQ, II (June, September, 1901), 119–167, 209–254.

Molson, Mrs. William M. "Glimpses of Life in Early Oregon." OHQ, I (June, 1900), 158–164.

Morrison, Dorothy and Morrison, Jean. "The Reluctant Fur Trader. Dr. John McLoughlin's Entry into the Fur Trade." OHQ. In press.

Nesmith, Col. J. W. "Address to the Oregon Pioneer Association, 1876." TOPA, 1880, 8–27.

*Ogden, Peter Skene. "Journals." OHQ, X, XI (December, 1909; June, December, 1910), 331–365; 201–222; 355–397.

*Ogden, Peter Skene, edited by Frederick Merk. "Report on the Snake Country Expedition." OHQ, XXXV (June, 1934), 93–122.

*"Old Letters from the Hudson Bay Company Officials and Employees from 1829–1840." From *Documents,* WHQ, I (July, 1907), 256–266.

**Oregon Spectator*, published Oregon City, February 5, 1846–January 7, 1854.

*Roberts, G. B., edited by Thomas Vaughan and Priscilla Knuth.

"The Round Hand of George B. Roberts . . ." OHQ, LXIII (June–September, 1962), 101–241.

Sage, Donald. "Swirl of Nations." *The Beaver*, Spring, 1963, 32–40.

*Schafer, Joseph, editor. "Documents Relative to Warre and Vavasour's Military Reconnaissance in Oregon, 1845–6." OHQ, X (March, 1909), 1–99.

*Schafer, Joseph, editor. "Letters of Sir George Simpson, 1841–1843." *American Historical Review*, XIV (October, 1908), 70–94.

Scott, Leslie M., editor. "Report of Lieutenant Peel on Oregon, 1845–46." OHQ, XXIX (March, 1928), 51–76.

Scott, Leslie M. "Modern Fallacies of Champoeg." OHQ, XXXII (September, 1931), 213–216.

*Slacum, Lieut. William. "Report on Oregon." OHQ, XIII (June, 1912), 176–224.

Thornton, Hon. J. Quinn. "History of the Provisional Government." TOPA, 1874, 43–96.

*Tolmie, Dr. William Frazer. "Journal." WHQ, III (July, 1912), 229–241.

Walker, Courtney M. "Sketch of Ewing Young." TOPA, 1880, 56–58.

Watt, Joseph. "Recollections of Dr. John McLoughlin." TOPA, 1886, 24–27.

*Wilkes, Charles. "Diary of Wilkes in the North West." WHQ, XVI (January, April, July, 1926), 49–61; 137–145; 206–223.

*Wilkes, Charles. "Report on the Territory of Oregon." OHQ, XII (September, 1911), 269–299.

Wilson, Clifford P. "The Beaver Club." *The Beaver*, March, 1936, 19–24.

*Work, John. "Journal." WHQ, III (July, 1912), 198–228; V (April, July, October, 1914), 83–115; 163–191; 258–277; VI (January, 1916), 26–49.

Index

Quotation Credits

Quoted by permission of the Bancroft Library, pages 51, 55, 94, 146

Fur Trade and Empire, revised edition, The Belknap Press of Harvard University Press, 1968, pages 35, 40, 43, 45–46

Hudson's Bay Record Society, Winnipeg, Canada for permission to quote from the McLoughlin letters.

McLoughlin Memorial Association, pages 3, 8, 14, 15, 19, 22, 25, 27, 46, 92, 93

Old Fort William, Thunder Bay, Ontario, page 8

Oregon Historical Society, pages 4, 86, 144, 149

Public Archives of Canada, page 26

University of British Columbia, pages 107, 110, 117

The Author

Dorothy Morrison spent her childhood in Nashua, Iowa, and attended the University of Northern Iowa and the State University of Iowa, where she received a bachelor's degree and did one year of graduate work in music. After two years of teaching, she married Dr. Carl V. Morrison, and moved to Portland, Oregon.

She has played violin with community orchestras, chamber groups, and the Portland Opera Orchestra, and is presently a member of the Chehalem Symphony Orchestra. Her other hobbies include photography, travel, needlework, square dancing, and most recently, swimming with the Masters' Swimming Program. She has traveled extensively in Mexico, Europe and the South Pacific.

With special interest in the history of the Northwest, she collects original books on that period. She is coauthor with Dr. Morrison of *Can I Help How I Feel?*, which deals with emotional problems of young people.

She has also written three other biographies related to the West:

Ladies Were Not Expected: Abigail Scott Duniway and Women's Rights, Chief Sarah: Sarah Winnemucca's Fight for Indian Rights, Under a Strong Wind: The Adventures of Jessie Benton Frémont

Following the death of Dr. Morrison in 1980, Mrs. Morrison married Robert C. Hunter, an attorney. They live on a forty-acre farm west of Portland.